64

5587

C. M. Ward
What You Should Know About
PROPHECY

C. M. Ward

What You Should Know About

PROPHECY

Adapted from *Bible Prophecy* by Stanley M. Horton

Gospel Publishing House/Springfield, Mo. 65802

02-0890

WHAT YOU SHOULD KNOW ABOUT PROPHECY
© 1975 by the Gospel Publishing House, Springfield, Missouri
65802. All rights reserved. Adapted from *Bible Prophecy* by
Stanley M. Horton, © 1963 by the Gospel Publishing House. Li-
brary of Congress Catalog No. 75-22610. ISBN 0-88243-890-5.
Printed in the United States of America.

A teacher's guide for individual or group study with this book is
available from the Gospel Publishing House. (Order number 32-
0164)

Contents

1 The Way God Speaks

Spiritual communication is different from anything else on earth. Heaven does report and share. "He revealeth his secrets unto his servants the prophets" (Amos 3:7).

God wants His plans and administration communicated correctly and authoritatively. He selected those who would not deviate. He chose *reporters*—not editors—for the task.

Before the Flood, God shared with Enoch a decision that still waits to be implemented—the return of His Son to earth, "with ten thousands of His saints" (Jude 14). In that knowledge he walked so close to God that God took him to heaven without his dying.

God talked to Moses "mouth to mouth" (Numbers 12:8). He had this testimony, that he was "faithful in all mine house" (Numbers 12:7). God leapfrogged centuries for His friend and showed him the manner of Christ's appearance upon earth, "of thy brethren, like unto me" (Deuteronomy 18:15). Moses, like Enoch, experienced arrangements of transfer from time to eternity.

Prophets are a special breed.

How Are They Selected?

God chooses. No one, on his or her own, decided to write a portion of the Bible.

Speaking God's message is the most coveted of all heaven's dispositions. "Covet to prophesy" (1 Corinthians 14:39).

The original writings of the Old and New Testament prophets are authoritative and unimpeachable. The prophet today speaks for God too, but these utterances do not have the same value as the Scriptures. Prophecy as a gift of the Spirit is the privilege of all Spirit-filled Christians (1 Corinthians 14:31).

The knowledge God desires to communicate is as present among mankind as is God himself. He simply chooses "servants" to state that message accurately.

Moses' intimacy with God led him to say, "Would God that all the Lord's people were prophets, and that the Lord would put his Spirit upon them!" (Numbers 11:29).

Samuel organized a school of the prophets. Elijah and Elisha organized similar schools. Charismatic fellowships grew everywhere after the Day of Pentecost.

Jeremiah was chosen. He was set apart in his mother's womb.

God occasionally commandeered. Some were reluctant. Jonah was. Others felt insufficient. "Then said I, Woe is me! for I am undone; because I am a man of unclean lips, and I dwell in the midst of a people of unclean lips" (Isaiah 6:5).

All whom God employed as prophets learned to lean totally upon the divine.

Christ exercised executive privilege. Out of many He chose twelve. "Ye have not chosen me, but I have chosen you" (John 15:16).

This mystifies a world system. God always has the situation in hand. He has already handpicked the tool of His will. "Separate me Barnabas and Saul for the work whereunto I have called them" (Acts 13:2).

God fits personality, experience, talent, ethnic background, and age differential to the task. He does not demand a stereotyped personality. He does not run everybody through a mold. God exercises faith in His partners.

The ones God has called and used form a galaxy of people.

There have been the brilliantly educated like Joseph, Moses, Isaiah, Jeremiah, Nehemiah, Paul, and Apollos. Others were chosen from obscure backgrounds. Gideon said, "Behold, my family is poor in Manasseh, and I am the least in my father's house" (Judges 6:15).

You can trust God's executive ability. One thing is certain, *He will never waste a life.*

How Does the Method Work?

It works through the transmission of the Holy Spirit. Truth is the ultimate goal. "He will guide you into all truth: for he shall not speak of himself; but whatsoever he shall hear, that shall he speak: and he will show you things to come" (John 16:13).

God has spoken to the subconscious. Joseph, Daniel, Ezekiel all reported the plan of God as they learned it by dream and vision. "And He put forth the form of a hand, and took me by a lock of mine head; and the spirit lifted me up between the earth and the heaven, and brought me in the visions of God to Jerusalem, to the door of the inner gate that looketh toward the north; where was the seat of the image of jealousy, which provoketh to jealousy" (Ezekiel 8:3).

God, by inner compulsion, has arrested the person

chosen. Amos shares his experience. "The lion hath roared, who will not fear? the Lord God hath spoken, who can but prophesy?" (Amos 3:8). You know when God is talking to you.

Jeremiah knew it. Circumstances were so unpleasant he wanted to quit. "I will not make mention of him, nor speak any more in his name." It didn't work out that way. God was too big for him. "But his word was in mine heart as a burning fire shut up in my bones, and I was weary with forebearing, and I could not stay" (Jeremiah 20:9).

NOT LIKE MEDIUMS OR OCCULT

God does not operate in a vacuum.

The Spirit clothes himself by the prophets.

God and man are tied in performance through the agency of the Spirit.

"And the Lord said unto Moses, Gather unto me seventy men of the elders of Israel, whom thou knowest to be the elders of the people, and officers over them; and bring them unto the tabernacle of the congregation, that they may stand there with thee. And I will come down and talk with thee there: and I will take of the spirit which is upon thee, and will put it upon them; and they shall bear the burden of the people with thee, that thou bear it not thyself alone" (Numbers 11:16,17).

Micah describes his experience. "Truly I am full of power by the spirit of the Lord." God's purpose for Micah was that he declare and come to grips with the sin of His people (Micah 3:8).

The servant is *overlaid*. Human personality is clothed upon.

NOT A TRANCE OR HYPNOSIS

The prophet or prophetess knew at all times what he or she was saying or doing. There is no similarity whatever to pagan incantation or the soothsayer.

God places the false prophet, or one who preys upon either the fears or expectations of mankind, in a serious category of crimes against humanity.

God works with and uses human intelligence.

Aaron was appointed high priest and it is recorded, "I will be with thy mouth, . . . and will teach you what ye shall do" (Exodus 4:15).

God permitted these designated "servants" to *see,* and they were often called "seers." The text they wrote was not fantasy. The enablement was provided by gifts of the Spirit in operation. These are the eternal reflexes extended toward mortality in a taste of things to come.

UTTERANCE BEYOND RHETORIC

When God called Isaiah, He touched his mouth. Isaiah describes his charismatic experience: "And he laid it upon my mouth, and said, Lo, this hath touched thy lips; and thine iniquity is taken away, and thy sin purged" (Isaiah 6:7).

These chosen ones became God's "mouth." That is why they so often spoke in the first person, "I say."

THE MESSAGE

Oratory is not prophecy.

A position paper is not prophecy.

An essay is not prophecy.

Prophecy is a direct and unabridged message.

God gave Jeremiah a message, not only for the

11

future, but for the people of his own day, for his neighbors. That message involved warning as well as encouragement. There was no human revision.

God did more than use Jeremiah's words. *He used his life.* He became God's illustration to that generation. God wrote the script in flesh. It became impossible either to ignore or to escape what God wanted understood.

Prophets are living "epistles."

God sees that Earth gets the "news"—"known and read of all men" (2 Corinthians 3:2).

There is in prophecy a confrontation. "Who also hath made us able ministers of the new testament; not of the letter, but of the spirit: for the letter killeth, but the spirit giveth life" (2 Corinthians 3:6).

"He that prophesieth speaketh unto men to edification, and exhortation, and comfort" (1 Corinthians 14:3).

PENALTY

Such extraordinary privilege carried extraordinary penalty for failure or compromise. This became an additional safeguard. Ezekiel was warned. "So thou, O son of man, I have set thee a watchman unto the house of Israel; therefore thou shalt hear the word at my mouth, and warn them from me" (Ezekiel 33:7).

TODAY

Unction and inspired utterance and mandate by the Holy Spirit are provided today so that the Bible, as it stands complete, may be preached as God intends it to be preached.

You and I have God's Word in our hands.

We no longer wait for God to speak. God waits for us to do so.

2 Defense Against Deceit

There are built-in safeguards.

"Believe not every spirit, but try the spirits whether they are of God" (1 John 4:1).

Moses anticipated forecasters and demagogues and special interests. "If there arise among you a prophet, or a dreamer of dreams, and giveth thee a sign or a wonder" (Deuteronomy 13:1), they were to follow the procedure God outlined for them.

A warning was sounded about enchanters, charmers, wizards. "And if thou say in thine heart, How shall we know the word which the Lord hath not spoken? when a prophet speaketh in the name of the Lord, if the thing follow not, nor come to pass, that is the thing which the Lord hath not spoken, but the prophet hath spoken it presumptuously: thou shalt not be afraid of him" (Deuteronomy 18:21,22).

You can put the Bible to every test.

A Position of Peril and Pinnacle

The moment I say, "Thus saith the Lord," I await the verdict, true or false.

Prophets accepted that peril.

They spoke when it was not popular to speak. It cost them their lives. They did not sit on ecclesiastical thrones dispensing mandates to the openmouthed.

They were rejected. Religious leaders denied the validity of their messages.

CORRUPT PRACTICES

Every culture, every ethnic group, has its diviners. The Canaanites were no exception.

It was a booby trap for Israel.

God warned about the custom of human sacrifice. The attraction could have been the chance to demonstrate their zeal in worship. "We do not hold back even our children from the demands of our gods."

Sincerity is never conclusive proof that you are right.

Canaan was soaked in religion. There were mediums, priests, astrologers everywhere. Their claims were loud that they could see and influence the future. They communed, they said, with the stars or with the dead, or with ancient script.

It was the devil's territory.

So God warned Israel!

SEDUCED BY FALSE PROPHETS

The blandishments often overwhelmed Israel. The dazzle and glamor of false prophets proved a subtle menace.

There were purges or reformations and a return to spiritual zeal intermittently. King Saul began with a housecleaning campaign. But his mind darkened from disobedience, and in the fading hours of his life he sought direction and comfort from the forbidden.

Elijah withstood 450 false prophets.

Their ranks replenish quickly.

Four hundred of them were assembled to mislead Jehoshaphat into an alliance with Ahab against Syria.

Wrong Counsel Leads to Bankruptcy

It was a trail for Israel that led to Babylonian captivity. Without direction from God, idolatry takes over. You become the prisoner of things and situations.

"Then the Lord said unto me, The prophets prophesy lies in my name: I sent them not, neither have I commanded them, neither spake unto them: they prophesy unto you a false vision and divination, and a thing of nought, and the deceit of their heart" (Jeremiah 14:14).

They promised peace and prosperity without repentance and righteousness.

Ezekiel was plagued by them in the midst of the captives at Babylon. "Woe unto the foolish prophets, that follow their own spirit, and have seen nothing!" (Ezekiel 13:3).

It's Always Big Business

Peter detected them. "There were false prophets also among the people even as there shall be false teachers among you" who will speak "great swelling words of vanity" (2 Peter 2:1,18).

Paul warns of these days. "In the latter times some shall depart from the faith, giving heed to seducing spirits, and doctrines of devils" (1 Timothy 4:1).

Who Will Speak Out?

The real enemy is public complacency.

People believe what they *want* to believe. It's a market that affords greedy trade.

Micah observes, "If a man walking in the spirit [wind] and falsehood do lie, saying, I will prophesy unto thee of wine and of strong drink [promoting self-indulgence]; he shall even be the prophet of this people" (Micah 2:11). He is saying the convenient thing, the thing the people want to hear.

He is a *populist*.

It puzzled Jeremiah.

"A wonderful and horrible thing is committed in the land; the prophets prophesy falsely, and the priests bear rule by their means; and my people love to have it so: and what will ye do in the end thereof?" (Jeremiah 5:30,31).

Paul gave a name to it: "itching ears."

WE NEED NOT BE DECEIVED

The Bible gives specific tests by which true prophets can be distinguished from the false.

There's a dramatic example in Jeremiah's confrontation.

After Nebuchadnezzar took King Jehoiakim and 10,000 Jewish captives to Babylon, Jeremiah urged the new king, Zedekiah, to acept the yoke of Babylon as God's discipline, lest further judgment come on the Jews.

Jeremiah prophesied that the yoke of Babylon would endure 70 years.

As an object lesson to headline his message, Jeremiah wore a wooden yoke on his neck.

Hananiah, a false prophet, ridiculed Jeremiah.

He said that God would break the yoke in two years.

In a flurry of zeal, Hananiah took the yoke from Jeremiah's neck and broke it.

Jeremiah's reply was that breaking wooden yokes had only made yokes of iron and that Judah *must* serve Babylon for the appointed time.

Then Jeremiah put it on the line.

He told Hananiah, "The Lord hath not sent thee; but thou makest this people to trust in a lie. Therefore thus saith the Lord; Behold, I will cast thee from off the face of the earth: this year thou shalt die, because thou hast taught rebellion against the Lord" (Jeremiah 28:15,16).

Here was the test!

Hananiah said that the captives would return within two full years. Jeremiah said that that year Hananiah would die. Time would determine one or the other to be a false prophet.

The facts fully vindicated Jeremiah. Hananiah did die that year, and the yoke of Babylon continued until Cyrus reigned in 536 B.C., long after Jeremiah passed from the scene of action.

THE PERCENTAGES

Someone in the business might predict some sign, some development, and by some coincidence, trick, or Satanic wrinkle have it come to pass—so a further test was necessary.

It was this.

No man, no matter how successful, if he turned the people away from the pure worship of the Lord, was to be considered a true prophet. God's Word is inviolate.

The ministry of a true prophet will draw people closer to God. The fruit of their ministry identifies them. "Ye shall know them by their fruits. Do men gather grapes of thorns, or figs of thistles?" (Matthew 7:16). "A good tree cannot bring forth evil fruit, neither can a corrupt tree bring forth good fruit" (Matthew 7:18).

A true prophet's ministry is always in keeping with the divine text. His teaching will never contradict the Bible.

We must compare Scripture portion with Scripture portion. It is the whole that counts. I should never build a doctrine or a movement on a fragment. I must always keep in mind that a *text* without *context* is a *pretext*.

"Though we, or an angel from heaven, preach any other gospel unto you than that which we have preached unto you, let him be accursed" (Galatians 1:8).

WILL POINT TO CHRIST

The Bible finds its unity in the bloodline that leads to Christ.

Any prophet who denies this is a false prophet who partakes of the spirit of the Antichrist.

So, watch it!

Is Jesus front and center? John "bare record of the word of God, and of the testimony of Jesus Christ, and of all things that he saw" (Revelation 1:2).

John was eternally disciplined by this guideline. "For I testify unto every man that heareth the words of the prophecy of this book, If any man shall add unto these things, God shall add unto him the plagues that are written in this book: and if any man shall take away from the words of the book of this prophecy, God shall take away his part out of the book of life, and out of the holy city, and from the things which are written in this book" (Revelation 22:18,19).

TWO CHECKPOINTS

First, will a prophecy line up with the Word.

Second, will a prophecy draw the listener closer to the Lord in a life that honors Him and Him alone?

Misplaced faith is mankind's greatest sorrow.

The "great faith" that pleased Jesus was always simple faith that trusted Him and believed His word.

TOLERANCE

The religious world peddles this with enthusiasm today. But toleration often becomes the indifference to both good and bad.

There is no substitute for truth.

False prophets are a menace, no matter how exciting.

3 The Proof Is in the Pudding

What makes a prophet?

Why is he different?

Elijah learned there were 7,000 in Israel faithful to God. He, however, was the only one who took an open, public stand for God.

He faced one of the most wicked women of all time, Jezebel. A prophet must often stand alone.

It is not meant to be a popular stance. A world system does not want God's message or God's man.

He, and his, are interpreted as "a stumblingblock," "foolishness," and belonging to a level of uninformed, underprivileged, and discredited humanity. They lack accreditation from society.

They are endorsed by a higher authority.

Paul speaks of his credentials. "And my speech and my preaching was not with enticing words of man's wisdom, but in demonstration of the Spirit and of power: that your faith should not stand in the wisdom of men, but in the power of God" (1 Corinthians 2:4,5).

THE FINGER OF GOD

God reminds mankind of His presence. He writes in miracle His true nature—merciful, compassionate, generous. The miracle calls public attention to His man, His woman, and His Word. This was the case with Moses.

There is always a Pharaoh, a Jezebel, a Pharisee.

They are determined to cancel the plan of God. They threaten and coerce. They are skilled and angry antagonists. They wish to substitute the way of the world, the flesh, and the devil.

The prophet is *God's umpire*. God places in the prophet authority to implement heaven's decision.

Elijah gave the Word and God backed it with fire. Elisha gave the Word and leprosy disappeared.

CONFIRMATION BY SIGNS

The believer is given the advantage of "signs."

"These signs shall follow them that believe" (Mark 16:17). The prophet is a spokesman, and it can be quickly determined for whom he is speaking.

Jesus said, "The same works that I do, bear witness of me" (John 5:36).

PRECISE TIMING

Joseph is unparalleled in history as an economist. He predicted accurately seven years of plenty and seven years of famine.

God always has His man or woman for the occasion.

Moses was God's answer to the interval of 400 years seen in vision by Abraham. "And he said unto Abram, Know of a surety that thy seed shall be a stranger in a land that is not theirs, and shall serve them; and they shall afflict them four hundred years" (Genesis 15:13).

So God furnished Moses to handle the exit.

VINDICATION

A prophet will be challenged viciously.

Korah, Dathan, On, and Abiram mutinied against Moses. They polished their reputation for spirituality and credibility. They made a bid for Israel's endorsement.

The question of leadership was at stake.

The challengers wanted to interpret God's law for selfish purposes. God's character was on the line.

Thus the unforgettable lesson and the vindication of Moses! "And Moses said, Hereby ye shall know that the Lord hath sent me to do all these works; for I have not done them of mine own mind. If these men die the common death of all men, or if they be visited after the visitation of all men; then the Lord hath not sent me. But if the Lord make a new thing, and the earth open her mouth, and swallow them up, with all that appertain unto them, and they go down quick into the pit; then ye shall understand that these men have provoked the Lord. And it came to pass, as he had made an end of speaking all these words, that the ground clave asunder that was under them: and the earth opened her mouth, and swallowed them up, and their houses, and all the men that appertained unto Korah, and all their goods. They, and all that appertained to them, went down alive into the pit, and the earth closed upon them: and they perished from among the congregation" (Numbers 16:28-33).

FULFILLED PROPHECY

Fulfilled prophecy encourages us to believe that the same God will fulfill unfulfilled prophecy.

The rationalist hedges by supplying a spiritual meaning. Prophecy is literal. Forgiveness is literal. Healing is literal. So is what God says about tomorrow. "This same Jesus . . . shall so come in like manner as ye have seen him go" (Acts 1:11).

The *past* is a witness to the *present*.

GOD PERFORMS WHAT HE PROMISES

God said Sarah would bear a son to Abraham. "And God said, Sarah thy wife shall bear thee a son indeed; and thou shalt call his name Isaac: and I will establish my covenant with him for an everlasting covenant, and with his seed after him" (Genesis 17: 19). And she did.

God said that He would protect Jeremiah from his enemies who wanted to kill him. "And they shall fight against thee; but they shall not prevail against thee; for I am with thee, saith the Lord, to deliver thee" (Jeremiah 1:19). And they did not. "But the king commanded Jerahmeel the son of Hammelech, and Seraiah the son of Azriel, and Shelemiah the son of Abdeel, to take Baruch the scribe and Jeremiah the prophet: but the Lord hid them" (Jeremiah 36:26).

History is written God's way.

Prophecy is history foretold—today's headlines written yesterday.

EGYPT

Egypt's power of empire in antiquity is unquestioned. Isaiah declared Assyria would conquer it. "So shall the king of Assyria lead away the Egyptians prisoners, and the Ethiopians captives, young and old, naked and barefoot, even with their buttocks uncovered, to the shame of Egypt" (Isaiah 20:4).

Isaiah saw that Egypt would become weak and lose its place of world leadership. "In that day shall Egypt be like unto women: and it shall be afraid and fear because of the shaking of the hand of the Lord of hosts, which he shaketh over it" (Isaiah 19:16). "For the Egyptians shall help in vain, and to no purpose: therefore have I cried concerning this, Their strength is to sit still" (Isaiah 30:7).

These were bold statements and not open to guesswork.

In 605 B.C. Nebuchadnezzar routed them completely and took over their Asiatic possessions.

In 525 B.C. Cambyses II, the son of Cyrus, made Egypt a Persian province.

In 332 B.C. Greece annexed Egypt.

In 30 B.C. it became Roman territory.

EGYPTIAN CITIES

The proud city of Thebes on the Nile, known in ancient times as No or No-Ammon, came under special indictment.

It was once a city of 100 gates. The ancient historian Tacitus declared it could mobilize an army of 700,000 men from its own population. The temple of Luxor and the 150 acres of magnificent columns, pillars, and temples at Karnak a mile down the river from Luxor were all part of ancient Thebes.

"And I will make Pathros desolate, and will set fire in Zoan, and will execute judgments in No. And I will pour my fury upon Sin, the strength of Egypt; and I will cut off the multitude of No. And I will set fire in Egypt: Sin shall have great pain, and No shall be rent asunder, and Noph shall have distresses daily" (Ezekiel 30:14-16).

Only the ancient ruins today speak of the former glory.

The word by Ezekiel, confirming Isaiah, was fulfilled. "And I will bring again the captivity of Egypt . . . and they shall be there a base kingdom" (Ezekiel 29:14).

Ezekiel saw down the corridors of time.

"And I will make the rivers dry, and sell the land into the hand of the wicked: and I will make the land waste, and all that is therein, by the hand of strangers: I the Lord have spoken it" (Ezekiel 30:12).

Judgment past is assurance of judgment future.

NINEVEH

God told Isaiah He was using the Assyrians as a rod to punish Israel and Judah.

Then in due time He would punish the Assyrians for their own sins.

Read this prophecy in the tenth chapter of Isaiah.

Zephaniah spoke further.

"And he will stretch out his hand against the north, and destroy Assyria; and will make Nineveh a desolation, and dry like a wilderness" (Zephaniah 2:13).

Assyria at that time was a land of gardens and orchards. Today it is arid.

Nahum spoke further.

"But with an overrunning flood he will make an utter end of the place thereof, and darkness shall pursue his enemies. What do ye imagine against the Lord? he will make an utter end: affliction shall not rise up the second time" (Nahum 1:8,9).

In 612 B.C. a combination of Medes, Scythians, and Babylonians besieged the city. Floodwaters of the rivers on two sides rose and tore a great section of the city wall. The invaders destroyed the city, and it was not rebuilt. It did not rise the second time.

This is a most amazing fact.

A Study in Contrast

One of the reasons archaeologists have such a wonderful time excavating the cities of the Middle East is that they were so often rebuilt. Another generation would level the ruins and build again. The archaeologist digs a trench through the accumulated ruins, and in the layers he finds a cross section of the city's history.

But not so Nineveh!

Nineveh was never rebuilt.

By the time of Alexander the Great the people who lived in that area had forgotten the location of the former world-capital. Not until about 1850 did Sir Austen Layard prove that a mound others had suspected to be Nineveh actually contained the remains of that city.

God's Word Is Final

"God, who at sundry times and in divers manners spake" (Hebrews 1:1).

The prophet is that instrument.

Jonah rebelled at the thought that what he foretold might not be fulfilled.

God wanted there to be a warning and an opportunity to repent. Jonah wanted judgment. He knew personally God's mercy, long-suffering, and love. God wanted the rest of the world to know what Jonah knew.

So the last move was God's.

Even the prophet could not change that.

Failure

Every attempt at empire building has fizzled. In our era Mussolini and Hitler have tried it. They did not succeed any more than the Caesars, Charlemagne, or Napoleon succeeded.

Every attempt at union by World Court, League of Nations, United Nations, or Common Market has shown crevices, the characteristics of iron and clay. "They shall not cleave one to another" (Daniel 2:43).

4 More Than a "Whodunit?"

Prophecy is more than a titillating "whodunit"— far more.

What distinguishes a man before God—money, brains, power, daring?

God looks on the *heart*.

Character is more important than cash.

God wants to restore His image in man that was marred in the Fall. He wants us to "put on the new man, which after God is created in righteousness and true holiness" (Ephesians 4:24).

God has such men and women.

THERE ARE ALWAYS CYNICS

There are those who shrug and say, "What is the use of studying about the Second Coming when there are so many differences of opinion about it? Why bother about such a controversial subject?"

Such an attitude makes the work of scoffers easier.

Indifference is a deadly virus.

So God finds men and women who speak out for Him.

HERE COME THE SCOFFERS

Who are they?

They peddle the old, worn merchandise that sees no room in nature or history for any divine intervention. They have shut God out of their lives, so they suppose that all nature does the same. They maintain that "all things continue as they were."

No position could be more stupid.

They imply that God has never brought the world to judgment and never will. They ignore the facts. They forget that God warned that a Flood would come, and in the days of Noah brought it to pass.

The ungodly do not like to think of either beginning or ending. They want to think of the now. The attack of man's treason against his God is focused against Genesis and the Revelation. He does not want to believe either. He wants a permissive God to sanction permissive living.

Remember! "All Scripture is given by inspiration of God, and is profitable for doctrine, for reproof, for correction, for instruction in righteousness" (2 Timothy 3:16).

God uses prophecy and its fulfillment for this purpose. "We have also a more sure word of prophecy; whereunto ye do well that ye take heed, as unto a light that shineth in a dark place, until the day dawn, and the day-star arise in your hearts" (2 Peter 1:19).

It is human nature to grow impatient. It leads to carelessness. The believer has been waiting for nearly 2,000 years. We need to remind ourselves that prophetic fulfillment has been experienced throughout this period of waiting.

TIME AS GOD COUNTS TIME

"But, beloved, be not ignorant of this one thing, that one day is with the Lord as a thousand years, and a thousand years as one day. The Lord is not slack concerning his promise, as some men count slackness; but is long-suffering to us-ward, not willing that any should perish, but that all should come to repentance" (2 Peter 3:8,9).

"And he [Jesus] said unto them, Go ye, and tell that fox [Herod], Behold, I cast out devils, and I do cures today and tomorrow, and the third day I shall be perfected" (Luke 13:32).

"After two days will he revive us: in the third day he will raise us up, and we shall live in his sight" (Hosea 6:2).

The *correct time* is by Israel and the Church.

The Messianic Hope of Israel and the Blessed Hope of the Church run parallel. Both are looking for the same Man.

It is evident, a world sign, that toward the close of the second millennium of the New Testament period— "after two days"—Hosea's nation of Israel has been "revived" or regathered, right on divine schedule.

The believer is on a two-day schedule as well. The purpose of the gospel is to "cast out devils, and do cures." That is the redemptive mission of Jesus.

A complete change, "the third day," is scheduled for both Israel and the Church.

DELAY

Delay strengthens trust.

Abraham was in the Promised Land 25 years before the promised son was born. Rebekah was barren for the first 20 years of her marriage with Isaac. Moses had to wait 40 years in the wilderness before God sent him back to fulfill the call to deliver Israel.

God therefore gives us enough in prophecy to encourage us and to guide us.

TIMES AND SEASONS

There is a lure to *speculate*.

It should be resisted lest the speculator add himself or herself to the long list of false prophets.

Some disciples asked, "Wilt thou at this time restore again the kingdom to Israel?" Jesus replied, "It is not for you to know the times or the seasons, which the Father hath put in his own power" (Acts 1:6,7).

The schedule is God's business.

Witnessing and spreading the gospel is man's business.

We have this target date: "And this gospel of the kingdom shall be preached in all the world for a witness unto all nations; and then shall the end come" (Matthew 24:14).

The best of all reasons to believe in the Second Coming is the First Coming. He came the first time on schedule and fulfilling every detail, such as the detail about his birth: "But thou, Bethlehem . . . though thou be little among the thousands of Judah, yet out of thee shall he come forth unto me that is to be ruler in Israel; whose goings forth have been from of old, from everlasting" (Micah 5:2).

ENOUGH

God does give us enough to reveal the broad sweep of His plan and to let us know He is in control.

GOD'S NOT PROCRASTINATING

God is not finding excuses for a growing interval of waiting. The plan is in operation. "But the day of the Lord will come." The resurrection guarantees it. "Because he hath appointed a day, in the which he will judge the world in righteousness by that man whom he hath ordained; whereof he hath given assurance unto all men, in that he hath raised him from the dead" (Acts 17:31).

God is sensitive to intercession.

God's partners have often obtained delays, and in some instances, reversals.

Amos, like Abraham, conducted business with God.

God showed Amos visions of a grasshopper plague and of fire. Amos prayed, and God did not send them. Then God showed Amos a vision of a plumb line. When a plumb line tests a wall and shows the wall is not perpendicular, the wall must come down. So God said, "I will not again pass by them any more" (Amos 7:8). God had set the day of reckoning. No amount of intercession would postpone it further.

WHEN WILL GOD DRAW THE LINE?

God reminded Jeremiah that He had faithfully sent prophets and warnings. There was no longer a response.

The word "end" is there on the pages of God's Book. There are deadlines. "Then said the Lord unto me, Though Moses and Samuel stood before me, yet my mind could not be toward this people: cast them out of my sight, and let them go forth" (Jeremiah 15:1).

The last message will be preached. The final invitation will be given. "Though these three men, Noah, Daniel, and Job, were in it, they should deliver but their own souls by their righteousness, saith the Lord God" (Ezekiel 14:14).

God himself retains the right to say, "It is finished!"

The Holy Spirit keeps the pressure where it should be kept. "Behold, now is the accepted time; behold, now is the day of salvation" (2 Corinthians 6:2).

You could give this meaning to the formula TNT—"Today not tomorrow."

Booby Traps Everywhere

The believer can be maimed. Satan has sown mine-fields filled with selfish interests. The believer must walk circumspectly with his eyes steadfastly upon Jesus. "Seeing then that all these things shall be dissolved, what manner of persons ought ye to be in all holy conversation and godliness" (2 Peter 3:11).

"Looking unto Jesus the author and finisher of our faith" (Hebrews 12:2). Peter learned this lesson in his bid to walk on water.

The warning to the believer is to be observant at all times—stay awake and alert. "Watch therefore: for ye know not what hour your Lord doth come" (Matthew 24:42).

We are not without *warning*. We are not without *witness*.

Big Things Ahead

That's why we ought to be big people.

There are big things ahead for Israel. God always provides *incentive*. God promises a flow of nations toward His glory in Israel. "I will gather all nations and tongues; and they shall come, and see my glory" (Isaiah 66:18).

Isaiah pleads with the nation to live up to this worthy goal. "O house of Jacob, come ye, and let us walk in the light of the Lord" (Isaiah 2:5).

Similarly!

"Every man that hath this hope in him purifieth himself, even as he is pure" (1 John 3:3).

Christ's return must be the influence which affects and directs my life.

If I live in victory now, I shall live in victory then.

Prophecy is given to focus attention.

5 The How of Interpretation

Can man *transmit* what God has to say?
Yes.
How?
"But God hath revealed them unto us by his Spirit: for the Spirit searcheth all things, yea, the deep things of God" (1 Corinthians 2:10).

"He shall glorify me: for he shall receive of mine, and shall show it unto you" (John 16:14).

REASON NOT ENOUGH

Human reason is the world's new god.
It is admirable.
It has its limits.
Start with a set of figures representing wave lengths of sound and you will end with charts and diagrams, but not with beautiful music. Start with a set of wave lengths of light and you may discover a fine theory, but not a fine painting. Figures and facts cannot bring beauty. Something additional must be added— experience.

Only the Holy Spirit provides sufficient dimension. Otherwise we are congested and shortsighted.

FOUNDATION

My premise must be a support better than mind or creed can provide. Reason and authority once said the earth did not move, that it was flat. Dissidents were imprisoned and flayed. A better knowledge of facts has proven the fundamentalists of former days were mistaken. Experience continues to cancel theory.

"Your faith should not stand in the wisdom of men, but in the power of God. Howbeit we speak wisdom among them that are perfect: yet not the wisdom of this world, nor of the princes of this world, that come to nought: but we speak the wisdom of God in a mystery, even the hidden wisdom, which God ordained before the world unto our glory" (1 Corinthians 2:5-7).

I must believe so that I shall never be ashamed.

Paul felt that way. "For I am not ashamed of the gospel of Christ: for it is the power [the authority, the experience] of God unto salvation to every one that believeth" (Romans 1:16).

That knowledge can never be exploded is a myth.

No Premium on Ignorance

Ignorance isn't faith.

Faith exceeds my perimeter of knowledge.

It isn't that God plays hide-and-seek. God makes every effort to reveal—the Bible, His Son, the Holy Spirit.

The moral rebel isn't anxious to learn.

"Because thou hast rejected knowledge, I will also reject thee" (Hosea 4:6).

"And this is the condemnation, that light is come into the world, and men loved darkness rather than light, because their deeds were evil. For every one that doeth evil hateth the light, neither cometh to the light, lest his deeds should be reproved" (John 3: 19,20).

These are the cases where the *wish* is father to the *thought*.

Science is a seeker, not an infallible guide.

THE EPHESIANS

In that sophisticated city of the Middle East a strange metamorphosis grew. People of that city discarded highly prized texts for the excellency of the Word. "So mightily grew the word of God and prevailed" (Acts 19:20).

The Bible is the prevailing force of Western growth and leadership. It is the Book upon which the President of the United States places his hand. It is prominent in our courts.

Everything that will stand the test of eternity rests upon it.

GUIDANCE

If you have something for which you seek guidance, go to the Word of God.

For instance, did God love all mankind, or only a select group? It was debated in the councils of men, but not in the councils of God. God spoke His will early. "In thee shall all families of the earth be blessed" (Genesis 12:3).

Paul learned by the Spirit that it wasn't necessary to become a Jew in order to become a believer. The door was Jesus and not circumcision.

THE BIBLE IS GOD-BREATHED

It isn't a classic put together by Shakespearian or Hemingway genius. The Holy Spirit gave birth as the Holy Spirit gave birth to the Babe of Bethlehem.

He did not permit academic liberties of tradition, speculation, or human opinion.

The Jews at Berea "searched the Scriptures daily, whether those things were so" (Acts 17:11). *The Word is the authority.*

"Trust in the Lord with all thine heart; and lean not unto thine own understanding. In all thy ways acknowledge him, and he shall direct thy paths" (Proverbs 3:5,6).

The Holy Spirit the Teacher

The Holy Spirit is the Vicar of Christ upon earth.

He is the Executive Administrator of Calvary's victory.

Jesus meant Him to be more than the respected companion of the knowledgeable evangelical. Jesus meant Him to be the resident chairman of the surrendered charismatic. "He that is *with* you shall be *in* you."

It is this "chaired ministry" through Christ's servants and handmaidens today that is equal to a world system's challenge. "And God hath set some in the church, first apostles, secondarily prophets, thirdly teachers, after that miracles, then gifts of healings, helps, governments, diversities of tongues" (1 Corinthians 12:28).

These are the conduits of this age.

They must be *checked.*

No man must set himself as supreme authority.

"Let the prophets speak two or three, and let the other judge" (1 Corinthians 14:29).

If the Bible were a textbook of theology, philosophy, or science, it would use word in a technical sense and each word would always have the same meaning.

But the Bible is God's Word in man's language.

That is important to remember.

We all use words that can have a different meaning depending on how and where we use them.

The mother who says she loves chocolate cake means something different by love than when she says she loves her baby. We have words with identical spelling and different meanings. *Light* can mean "not heavy" or "not dark." *Lead* pronounced one way is a metal, pronounced another way is a verb. When written you must examine the context to determine what is intended.

It is dangerous to take a half verse here and a half verse there and build a theory.

That will lead to twisted minds and twisted lives.

THE WHOLE

The skill required is: "Study to show thyself approved unto God, a workman that needeth not to be ashamed, rightly dividing the word of truth" (2 Timothy 2:15).

We must compare passage with passage.

We must seek God's *total view*.

The Holy Spirit will help. He furnishes illumination—"The eyes of your understanding being enlightened" (Ephesians 1:18).

A "workman" is required. There is no provision for the lazy. It takes study and prayer. Otherwise the avenues are closed.

The answers are in that Book.

The Holy Spirit will guide us to them.

This is the constant source of squabbles.

What hath God said?

Augustine said, "The *new* [New Testament] is in the *old* [Old Testament] concealed. The old is by the new revealed."

God chose and recorded illustrations.

These are stories, historical and biographical accounts, convenient patterns, teaching helps, incorporated in the Bible. They are there to explain and drive home spiritual truths.

Oil, for example, is sometimes a type of the Holy Spirit, sometimes of joy, and sometimes it is just oil, not a type at all.

"Knowing this first, that no prophecy of the Scripture is of any private interpretation. For the prophecy came not in old time by the will of man: but holy men of God spake as they were moved by the Holy Ghost" (2 Peter 1:20,21).

MISTAKEN INTERPRETATION

Repeatedly those have arisen who claim the Word is his or her total source, but that he or she is the only reliable custodian of interpretation.

Beware!

The Pharisees raised tradition to the level of truth.

In so doing they evangelized error which Jesus revealed in their postulates. Then they hated Jesus.

They told the disciples of Jesus that He could not be the Messiah because Malachi prophesied that Elijah must come first.

Jesus said they should know that Elijah had come already. The Word meant that a prophet should precede Christ whose message and ministry were similar to Elijah's. "The voice of him that crieth in the wilderness, Prepare ye the way of the Lord, make straight in the desert a highway for our God" (Isaiah 40:3). John the Baptist fulfilled this mission.

PICTURE LANGUAGE

God uses picture language. This is so important to remember when you read the Book of Revelation. Look at the picture! Then seek its meaning.

Jesus, in applying eternal truth to majestic simplicity used constantly the four-letter word "like." He always went from the *known* to the *unknown*. "The kingdom of heaven is like. . . ."

Thus the Book of Revelation may use the figure of a beast to describe the Antichrist. The beast in reality is a man with an unrestrained, brutish nature.

God adjusts himself to the limitations and inadequacies of human language. New words and usages are added to the vocabulary. And the Book of Revelation attempts, in the language then afforded, to describe events yet to take place.

So many lose the way amid symbols and figures of speech.

Stay with the central truth.

My suggestion is to make a practice of avoiding extravagant interpreters.

These usually have some form of "box office" in mind.

TIME IS PROPHECY'S ALLY

We can expect the interpretation of prophecy to become clearer as it is being fulfilled.

Isaiah 61 records prophecies referring to both the

first and second appearances of Jesus without indicating the time gap between.

I can understand the passage much better than the person living in Isaiah's day.

Jesus pointed to that passage when He spoke at Nazareth. He stopped abruptly when He came to the phrase "the day of vengeance of our God." He knew that portion belonged to His second appearance.

Be *bold* but not *dogmatic*.

Time affords a better insight.

6 The Central Figure

All Bible prophecy is a testimony to Jesus Christ. Jesus said so.

"And beginning at Moses and all the prophets, he expounded unto them in all the Scriptures the things concerning himself" (Luke 24:27).

The Old Testament points ahead to the first and second comings of Christ. The New Testament describes the first coming and looks ahead to the second.

You start within the first several pages of your Bible. "And I will put enmity between thee and the woman, and between thy seed and her seed; it shall bruise thy head, and thou shalt bruise his heel" (Genesis 3:15).

The "seed of the woman" is the big story of the Bible—the Virgin Birth.

The last book of the Bible, the Revelation, provides a look at the victorious Lamb. "And I beheld, and, lo, in the midst of the throne and of the four beasts, and in the midst of the elders, stood a Lamb as it had been slain" (Revelation 5:6).

Victory has been accomplished. That is the story of Isaac in type. "And she shall bring forth a son, and thou shalt call his name Jesus: for he shall save his people from their sins" (Matthew 1:21).

The sacrifice at Calvary is sufficient. *The debt is paid and cancelled.*

CONFLICT

The Israeli *preachers* of the Old Testament clearly identified the Messiah to come. The evidence is beyond reasonable doubt. It is conclusive. The Israeli *politicians* of the New Testament identified a different Messiah and determined to have a different Messiah. They created an image of successful warrior-leader returning political ascendancy to Israel. It was a death of Roman occupation they preferred rather than an atonement for personal trespass.

THE CROSS BEFORE THE CROWN

It had to be.

Messiah must first suffer, then reign.

Joseph is a true picture.

Isaiah set forth the plan of redemption accurately in the 53rd chapter of his prophecy.

Zechariah shows Joshua, the priest, in stained garments as a representative of the people. Satan opposes him, but he is given new, clean garments (Zechariah 3:1-8).

He is first *priest,* or intercessor, then *king,* or ruler.

This order is fixed in every Old Testament shadow of New Testament fulfillment.

POSITIVELY IDENTIFIED

The Old Testament provided so many checkpoints that no imposter could have survived. What man could order the events leading to and surrounding his death when they involved a great many people and when he would be under arrest or hanging on a cross?

Here, as listed by Dr. Stanley Horton, are some of these Old Testament checkpoints:

1. Betrayed by a friend (Psalm 55:12-14; 41:9; Mathew 26:46-50; John 13:18).

2. Sold for 30 pieces of silver (Zechariah 11:12; Matthew 26:14,15).

3. Money obtained to be cast to the potter (Zechariah 11:13; Matthew 27:3-10).

4. To be accused by false witnesses (Psalm 35:11; 109:2; Matthew 26:59,60).

5. Disciples to forsake Him (Zechariah 13:7; Maththew 26:56; Mark 14:27).

6. Smitten and spat upon the face (Isaiah 50:4-6; Luke 22:64; Matthew 26:67,68).

7. To be dumb before accusers (Isaiah 53:7; Matthew 27:12-14; 1 Peter 2:23).

8. To be wounded and bruised (Isaiah 53:5; Matthew 27:26-29).

9. To fall under the cross (Psalm 109:24; John 19:17; Luke 23:26).

10. Hands and feet to be pierced (Psalm 22:16; Luke 23:33; John 20:25-27).

11. To be crucified with thieves (Isaiah 53:12; Mark 15:27,28).

12. To pray for His persecutors (Isaiah 53:12; Psalm 109:4; Luke 23:34).

13. People to shake heads (Psalm 109:25; 22:7; Matthew 27:39).

14. People to ridicule Him (Psalm 22:8; Matthew 27:41,43).

15. People to stare astonished (Psalm 22:17; Isaiah 52:14; Luke 23:35).

16. Garments parted and lots cast (Psalm 22:18; John 19:23,24).

17. To cry, "My God, my God, why hast thou forsaken me?" (Psalm 22:1; Matthew 27:46).

18. To be offered gall and vinegar (Psalm 69:21; Mathew 27:34; John 19:28,29).

19. To commit himself to God (Psalm 31:5; Luke 23:46).

20. Friends to stand afar off (Psalm 38:11; Luke 23:49).

21. Bones not to be broken (Psalm 34:20, noting that the Passover lamb was not to have its bones broken and Christ is our Passover Lamb; Exodus 12:46; 1 Corinthians 5:7).

22. His side to be pierced (Zechariah 12:10; John 19:34,37).

23. His heart to be broken (Psalm 22:14; John 19:34).

24. Darkness to cover the land (Amos 8:9; Matthew 27:45).

25. Buried in a rich man's tomb (Isaiah 53:9; Matthew 27:57-60).

Someone has figured out that the probability of all these things happening at once is once in 33 million, and the possibility of all these things being fulfilled in any one person at the same time is almost inconceivable. Yet even though they were predicted anywhere from 400 to 2,000 years before they happened, they all fitted perfectly. After Jesus pointed the disciples to these things they realized that the Cross was not a mistake or a tragic martyrdom which might have been avoided but a vital part of God's plan (Acts 2:23; 4:28; Galatians 1:4; Revelation 13:8; 1 Peter 1:20).

No Loopholes

Old Testament prophecy provides no options.

It narrows possibilities until Jesus of Nazareth is *fact, fiction,* or *fraud.*

He must come through Shem's descendants. "Blessed be the Lord God of Shem" (Genesis 9:26).

The focus turns to Abraham. "Seeing that Abraham shall surely become a great and mighty nation, and all the nations of the earth shall be blessed in him" (Genesis 18:18).

Then in selectivity, the indicator moves toward one tribe, Judah. "The sceptre shall not depart from Judah, nor a lawgiver from between his feet, until Shiloh come; and unto him shall the gathering of the people be" (Genesis 49:10).

And in the tribe of Judah, one man is segregated, David.

"And when thy days be fulfilled, and thou shalt sleep with thy fathers, I will set up thy seed after thee, which shall proceed out of thy bowels, and I will establish his kingdom. He shall build a house for my name, and I will stablish the throne of his kingdom for ever. I will be his father, and he shall be my son. If he commit iniquity, I will chasten him with the rod of men, and with the stripes of the children of men: but my mercy shall not depart away from him, as I took it from Saul, whom I put away before thee. And thine house and thy kingdom shall be established for ever before thee: thy throne shall be established for ever" (2 Samuel 7:12-16).

More Details

Here are some examples:

He was to be born of a *virgin*. "Therefore the Lord himself shall give you a sign; Behold, a virgin shall conceive, and bear a son, and shall call his name Immanuel" (Isaiah 7:14).

He was to be born in *Bethlehem*. "But thou, Bethlehem Ephratah, though thou be little among the thousands of Judah, yet out of thee shall he come forth unto me that is to be ruler in Israel; whose goings forth have been from of old, from everlasting" (Micah 5:2).

He was to have a humble yet triumphal *entry* into Jerusalem. "Rejoice greatly, O daughter of Zion; shout, O daughter of Jerusalem: behold, thy King cometh unto thee: he is just, and having salvation; lowly, and riding upon an ass, and upon a colt the foal of an ass" (Zechariah 9:9).

The infidel hasn't any case.

INTERMINGLED

Israeli preachers saw Christ's second coming as well as the first. Furthermore, God wrote the story across Israeli history.

Joseph was repudiated by his brethren. Later he became their savior and ruler.

Moses was rejected by his brethren. Later he was their savior and leader.

David was discounted by his nation. Later he was their happy choice and champion.

Ezekiel, Isaiah, Daniel, Zechariah, and Malachi are examples of prophets who spoke intelligently and boldly of Christ's second coming.

Daniel says, "and in a kingdom which shall not be destroyed."

Zechariah tells how He shall return to earth. His

feet will stand on the Mount of Olives causing it to split in half leaving a great valley running from east to west (Zechariah 14:4 and Ezekiel 43:2-4).

Your Faith Is Not Misplaced

You do not believe in Jesus in vain. Your confession that He is the only begotten Son of God is your saving confession.

"To him that overcometh will I grant to sit with me in my throne, even as I also overcame, and am set down with my Father in his throne" (Revelation 3: 21).

There are 260 chapters in the New Testament. In these chapters there are 318 references to Christ's return.

There is not a Christian doctrine that receives more attention in the Word of God than the second coming of Christ.

It should be *preached*.

7 The Big Promise

So much of it began with Abraham.

The word *faith* takes on meaning.

Paul pays tribute.

"Therefore it is of faith, that it might be by grace; to the end the promise might be sure to all the seed; not to that only which is of the law, but to that also which is of the faith of Abraham; who is the father of us all, (as it is written, I have made thee a father of many nations,) before him whom he believed, even God, who quickeneth the dead, and calleth those things which be not as though they were: who against hope believed in hope, that he might become the father of many nations, according to that which was spoken, So shall thy seed be. And being not weak in faith, he considered not his own body now dead, when he was about a hundred years old, neither yet the deadness of Sarah's womb: he staggered not at the promise of God through unbelief; but was strong in faith, giving glory to God; and being fully persuaded, that what he had promised, he was able also to perform. And therefore it was imputed to him for righteousness" (Romans 4:16-22).

That is like being awarded the Congressional Medal of Honor.

Yet Abraham's blessing is available to all. "Now it was not written for his sake alone, that it was imputed to him; but for us also, to whom it shall be imputed, if we believe on him that raised up Jesus our Lord from the dead" (Romans 4:23,24).

The *big message* is this. Faith pleases God. Abraham pleased God when he obeyed and "went out, not knowing whither he went" (Hebrews 11:8).

He didn't ask questions. He *trusted*.

This is God's requirement.

"There is no man that hath left house, or parents, or brethren, or wife, or children, for the kingdom of God's sake, who shall not receive manifold more in this present time, and in the world to come life everlasting" (Luke 18:29,30).

God has posted this reward.

Righteousness is an act of faith. It is more than knowledge or debate.

WHY ABRAHAM?

God called Abraham to be the source of a plan that would close the breach between mankind and himself. Israel was selected as the conduit. It was the task of Israel to prepare the way for the Redeemer.

God will not forget them for this.

When God spoke to Abraham mankind was *infected* and *affected* by sin. Sin is rebellion. It is the creature saying, "I won't" to the Creator.

Sin is:

"All unrighteousness is sin" (1 John 5:17). There is an eternal difference between *right* and *wrong*. God is always right.

"Sin is the transgression of the law" (1 John 3:4). There are no *little* sins any more than a woman can be a little pregnant. I am in violation whether I run a traffic light or commit armed robbery.

"Therefore to him that knoweth to do good, and doeth it not, to him it is sin" (James 4:17). Sin is being an accomplice.

"And he that doubteth is damned if he eat, because he eateth not of faith: for whatsoever is not of faith is sin" (Romans 14:23). Sin is failure to give God the benefit of the doubt.

"For all have sinned, and come short of the glory of God" (Romans 3:23). Sin is not being good enough. I am not generous enough. I am not forgiving enough. I am not kind enough. I need a lot to be added.

Calvary alone is that plus sign.

That was the indictment when God spoke to Abraham.

The Virus Hadn't Taken Long to Spread

Somehow it had stowed in the Ark. It quickly tainted the new start. "Cush begat Nimrod: he began to be a mighty one in the earth. He was a mighty rebel before the Lord . . . and the beginning of his kingdom was Babel" (Genesis 10:8-10).

It didn't take long for rebellion to focus. "Let us build . . . a city and a tower . . . and let us make us a name" (Genesis 11:4).

The *outside man,* the flesh, wants to build here for time. The *inside man,* the spirit, wants to build for eternity. "For the flesh lusteth against the Spirit, and the Spirit against the flesh: and these are contrary the one to the other; so that ye cannot do the things that ye would" (Galaians 5:17).

Paul tells the Colossians, "Set your affection on things above, not on things on the earth" (3:2). The love of property is strong temptation.

The "tower" is in contrast to the "ladder." Jacob

saw help furnished by God and divine assistance. Mankind has lofty aspirations. Human society—"Let *us* build"—wants to accomplish these worthwhile aspirations in and through and by man alone. "Because that, when they knew God, they glorified him not as God" (Romans 1:21).

Human pride and contest forever strive through trade name, service organization, denominational status, ethnic boasting, union organization, fraternity and sorority, family, athletic achievement, endlessly. There's always the attempt to be somebody as well as to possess something.

God says, "That at the name of Jesus every knee should bow, of things in heaven, and things in earth, and things under the earth" (Philippians 2:10). His name is above every name.

PUNISHMENT IS NOT THE ANSWER

The Flood could not bring the transformation the world needed. Neither could culture and education bring peace.

God moved toward man's need.

He chose an avenue of faith.

He offered a covenant or *contract* to Abraham. "And I will bless them that bless thee, and curse him that curseth thee: and in thee shall all families of the earth be blessed" (Genesis 12:3).

That contract is in force. It has never been revised or abrogated. God constantly strengthened that contract with Abraham, Isaac, and Jacob, *building faith* —victorious faith.

In His vision to Jacob, God let Jacob know that heaven was accessible to Jacob, and that God had provided a way.

Jesus defined "the ladder" and all that it is meant to be. "Hereafter ye shall see heaven open, and the angels of God ascending and descending upon the Son of Man" (John 1:51).

Heaven is open and "ministering spirits" are our daily benefactors. That is better than any earth struggle.

SPELLED OUT FOR ABRAHAM

God gave Abraham specifics.

"Unto thy seed have I given this land, from the river of Egypt unto the great river, the river Euphrates" (Genesis 15:18).

At Bethel God officially recognized Jacob as the heir of promise.

When Jacob blessed Joseph's sons, Jacob showed he had never lost sight of the promise, for he told Joseph, "I die; but God shall be with you, and bring you again into the land of your fathers" (Genesis 48:21). Joseph was a *believer*.

His exalted position never compromised his faith.

He said, "I die; and God will surely visit you, and bring you out of this land unto the land which he sware to Abraham, to Isaac, and to Jacob" (Genesis 50:24). Joseph made provision for his bones to be taken to the Promised Land when Israel returned.

Thus through almost 400 years of Egyptian residence, most of it in bondage, the bones of Joseph in their midst remained as a witness of God's promise.

Generations might die, *but God is not dead.*

His plan is operative.

Likewise:

"The dead in Christ shall rise first: then we which are alive and remain shall be caught up together with them in the clouds, to meet the Lord in the air" (1 Thessalonians 4:16,17).

"These all died in faith, not having received the promises, but having seen them afar off, and were persuaded of them, and embraced them, and confessed that they were strangers and pilgrims on the earth" (Hebrews 11:13).

His Faith Was Redeemed

"And Moses took the bones of Joseph with him: for he had straitly sworn the children of Israel, saying, God will surely visit you; and ye shall carry up my bones away hence with you" (Exodus 13:19).

Joseph exercised *faith*.

"And the bones of Joseph, which the children of Israel brought up out of Egypt, buried they in Shechem, in a parcel of ground which Jacob bought of the sons of Hamor the father of Shechem for an hundred pieces of silver; and it became the inheritance of the children of Joseph" (Joshua 24:32).

Moses Called

Again God chose!

The plan became bolder by type and example.

There would be the *Deliverer*.

The status of that land promised to Abraham has always been an integral, visible part of God's eternal contract. That is why it is the eye of the storm. It is a magnificent, continuing witness. It says through history written that no power on earth, or under the earth, can wrest it from the purpose ordained—to be tied to the birth, the residence, the coming again of His Son.

God's timeclock moves when Israel, as a nation, is in the land.

Hell, again, is busy trying to push the nation into the Mediterranean, trying to purge the land of the Jew, and thus strike at the covenant.

It is the *insanity* of history.

"For I will set mine eyes upon them for good, and I will bring them again to this land: and I will build them, and not pull them down; and I will plant them, and not pluck them up" (Jeremiah 24:6).

SEED MULTIPLIED

God said to Abraham, "And thy seed shall be as the dust of the earth; and thou shalt spread abroad to the west, and to the east, and to the north, and to the south" (Genesis 28:14).

Muliplication!

Abraham fathered Isaac.

Isaac begat two, Esau and Jacob.

Jacob begat twelve.

"Many shall come from the east and west, and shall sit down with Abraham, and Isaac, and Jacob, in the kingdom of heaven" (Matthew 8:11).

Israel has been scattered and has provided every nation on earth, where Israel has been temporary resident, brilliance, scientific breakthrough, economic discovery and advance. "And thou shalt become an astonishment, a proverb, and a byword, among all nations whither the Lord shall lead thee" (Deuteronomy 28:37).

But always, everywhere, the look is homeward.

"And among these nations shalt thou find no ease, neither shall the sole of thy foot have rest: but the Lord shall give thee there a trembling heart, and failing eyes, and sorrow of mind: and thy life shall hang in doubt before thee; and thou shalt fear day and night, and shalt have none assurance of thy life" (Deuteronomy 28:65,66).

If you doubt the accuracy of Bible prophecy, read the history of the Jews. *Could it have been foretold any more expressly?*

ISRAEL IS FOR EVERYBODY

"And in thee and in thy seed shall all the families of the earth be blessed" (Genesis 28:14).

How?

Through Jesus Christ.

The heartache of Israel made Paul weep:

"For I could wish that myself were accursed from Christ for my brethren, my kinsmen according to the flesh: who are Israelites; to whom pertaineth the adoption, and the glory, and the covenants, and the giving of the law, and the service of God, and the promises; whose are the fathers, and of whom as concerning the flesh Christ came, who is over all, God blessed forever. Amen" (Romans 9:3-5).

Israel's tragedy and her eventual triumph is portrayed in one of her preachers, Jonah.

Her mission to the Gentiles is, "Preach unto it the preaching that I bid thee" (Jonah 3:2). Israel's anguish will subside when she obeys that command.

God chose the territory of Canaan to be a beachhead in His battle against earth's idolatry and disobedience. *Through Israel God meant to keep the truth alive.*

God commissioned Israel a steward of His grace.

This is evident from the start.

God never intended Israel to be *exclusive.*

Israel always had included in God's headline of compliance an attitude toward the neighbor, expressed

56

again and again next to the first commandment of un-
adulterated love to himself—"Thou shalt love him
[the foreigner] as thyself" (Leviticus 19:34).

GRACE IS INCLUSIVE

The Book of Joshua shows how Rahab, a harlot, by
an exercise of faith in God's covenant, escaped the
curse of Canaan. She came into the camp of Israel
and enjoyed the full blessing. She became an ances-
tress of Jesus. See Matthew 1:5.

Ruth the Moabitess enjoyed the same privilege.

When God delivered the Jews through Mordecai
and Esther, we read that because of a godly fear of
the Jews "many of the people of the land became
Jews" (Esther 8:17).

It is interesting to look ahead.

Ezekiel speaks of millennial provision.

He says that any Gentile who wishes to enjoy the
blessing of a particular tribe may do so. Room will be
made for him, and he will be given a full inheritance.
"And it shall come to pass, that ye shall divide it by
lot for an inheritance unto you, and to the strangers
that sojourn among you, which shall beget children
among you: and they shall be unto you as born in the
country among the children of Israel; they shall have
inheritance with you among the tribes of Israel. And
it shall come to pass, that in what tribe the stranger
sojourneth, there shall ye give him his inheritance,
saith the Lord God" (Ezekiel 47:22,23).

A selfishness must be cleansed.

That is the story, the fulfillment, just ahead.

"Behold, at that time I will undo all that afflict
thee: and I will save her that halteth, and gather her
that was driven out; and I will get them praise and
fame in every land where they have been put to

shame. At that time will I bring you again, even in the time that I gather you: for I will make you a name and a praise among all people of the earth, when I turn back your captivity before your eyes, saith the Lord" (Zephaniah 3:19,20).

JESUS THE SEED

Jesus himself is the true Seed of Abraham.

There can be no argument.

"Now to Abraham and his seed were the promises made. He saith not, And to seeds, as of many; but as of one. And to thy seed, which is Christ" (Galatians 3:16).

That says it in one verse.

Isaac was *a* promised son but not *the* Promised Son.

The *silhouette* was there. It was a promise of things to come. Abraham's willingness to lay Isaac on the altar pointed to the love of the Father. Isaac's restoration at the point of death speaks volumes. The story of the *substitute* is there. Abraham acknowledged a revelation of God's nature. That recognition states that God understands the need of mankind and provides His own sacrifice to undertake for that need.

"By faith Abraham, when he was tried, offered up Isaac: and he that had received the promises offered up his only begotten son, of whom it was said, That in Isaac shall thy seed be called: accounting that God was able to raise him up, even from the dead: from whence also he received him in a figure" (Hebrews 11:17-19).

The New Testament certifies that the Seed is Jesus. "Ye are the children of the prophets, and of the covenant which God made with our fathers, saying unto Abraham, And in thy seed shall all the kindreds of the earth be blessed. Unto you first God, having raised up his Son Jesus, sent him to bless you, in turning away every one of you from his iniquities" (Acts 3: 25,26).

JACOB A PICTURE OF ISRAEL

God's dealings with Jacob are illustrative of His dealings with the Jews. It was foretold that they would be scattered, but it was also foretold that God's purpose was not destruction. God's purpose was to sift them, to purify them. "For, lo, I will command, and I will sift the house of Israel among all nations, like as corn is sifted in a sieve, yet shall not the least grain fall upon the earth" (Amos 9:9).

They were never to lose their identity.

WHAT DANIEL LEARNED

Daniel learned that the close of the 70 years of Babylonian captivity of Israel had not finished God's dealings with Israel.

Seventy weeks were determined.

They would be necessary to bring Israel to repentance, salvation, and righteousness, and fulfill God's plan for them. This description of a time element is heaven's standard of measurement. It is further divided. The first period consists of seven sevens. The second period consists of 62 sevens. The third period consists of a single seven, or "the seventieth week."

They were measured for certain purposes.

The start was tied to the commandment to restore and build Jerusalem. Sixty-nine sevens would bring the appearance of the Messiah Prince of Israel who would be cut off, but not for himself.

The last period is ominous.

In this period another prince will appear, the Great Deceiver. This period is marked by a firm covenant between the second prince and the Jewish nation, a covenant that he will break in the middle of that period.

Antichrist is coming.

Paul Sees It Happening at the Close of the Church Age

"And they also, if they abide not still in unbelief, shall be graffed in; for God is able to graff them in again" (Romans 11:23).

The sifting will be complete.

"For I would not, brethren, that ye should be ignorant of this mystery, lest ye should be wise in your own conceits, that blindness in part is happened to Israel, until the fulness of the Gentiles be come in" (Romans 11:25).

God's plan is being perfected.

In dealing with the times and seasons of Daniel's prophecy we must not forget the purpose of God to bring restoration, not merely to the land, *but to himself.*

This is foreshadowed at Sinai.

There God revealed that this was His purpose in delivering Israel from Egypt. "Ye have seen what I did unto the Egyptians, and how I bare you on eagles' wings, and brought you unto myself" (Exodus 19:4).

But Israel forgot.

Israel violated the covenant of Sinai .

God promised *a new covenant* that would provide forgiveness and real knowledge of God with a new heart and spirit. So many of the prophets take up this theme. "Then will I sprinkle clean water upon you, and ye shall be clean: from all your filthiness, and from all your idols, will I cleanse you. A new heart also will I give you, and a new spirit will I put within you: and I will take away the stony heart out of your flesh, and I will give you a heart of flesh. And I will put my spirit within you, and cause you to walk in my statutes, and ye shall keep my judgments, and do them" (Ezekiel 36:25-27).

GOD'S ORDER

Paul explains it.

"That was not first which is spiritual, but that which is natural; and afterward that which is spiritual" (1 Corinthians 15:46).

So the divine order is:

1. The political rebirth of Israel.
2. The spiritual rebirth of Israel.

The second will take place as certainly as the first.

This answers the question that asks why does God establish and sustain miraculously a nation that is so antichrist.

WHAT HAPPENS TO UNSAVED JEWS?

Faith is the one means of salvation.

Abraham's contract is implemented through Christ. Calvary funded that agreement.

Christ rejecting Jews is no different from Christ rejecting Russians or Christ rejecting Americans.

Those who enjoy the blessings of Abraham must have the resurrection faith Abraham had. "And if ye be Christ's, then are ye Abraham's seed, and heirs according to the promise" (Galatians 3:29).

Paul told the Romans, "For the promise, that he should be heir of the world, was not to Abraham, or to his seed, through the law, but through the righteousness of faith" (Romans 4:13).

And in verse 16 of the same chapter we read, "Therefore it is of faith, that it might be by grace; to the end the promise might be sure to all the seed; not to that only which is of the law, but to that also which is of the faith of Abraham; who is the father of us all."

So Jews are saved or lost the same way all of us are saved or lost.

None can avoid the question and personal decision: What will I do with Jesus of Nazareth—Is He or is He not the Only Begotten Son of God?

A vote is mandatory.

8 Jesus' Sermon About Signs

Matthew 24 and Luke 21 report what Jesus said would be *signs* of His return.

Speculation is dangerous.

It is the soil from which false prophets rise.

Absolutes are certain.

Like the definition of a straight line. "The shortest distance between two given points" is an absolute. That will not change.

There are absolutes in these passages.

"This gospel of the kingdom shall be preached in all the world for a witness unto all nations; and then shall the end come" (Matthew 24:14).

The "gospel of the kingdom" is not the social, liberal gospel of the present-day left. It is the authority of Jesus Christ who challenges and replaces the kingdom of darkness in man by the "divine nature." The "shalls" are unqualified. *The witness will be worldwide.*

Here is another absolute!

"This generation (race) shall not pass, till all these things be fulfilled" (Matthew 24:34)

Scofield translates the word *generation* "race." Jesus speaks of the Jewish people. Heinous attempts have been made to erase these people. They cannot succeed.

So watch the Church and watch Israel!

Jesus Taught He Would Go Away

He compared himself to a nobleman. He said the nobleman "went into a far country to receive for himself a kingdom, *and to return*" (Luke 19:12)

No true child of God should be taken unawares. "Ye, brethren, are not in darkness, that that day should overtake you as a thief" (1 Thessalonians 5:4).

There are traps for the Christian. Jesus named them undisciplined living (surfeiting) and anxiety (cares of this life). These can interfere with daily, sensitive observation of an eroding world system.

Endurance

If there is anything you can read in these two chapters it is that there can be no Millennium until Christ returns. Man cannot produce the perfect state.

Man cannot solve the problems of war, distribution, disease, or bigotry.

An important time phrase is "the beginning of sorrows" (Matthew 24:8).

"Distress of nations"

"Perplexity"

"Failing for fear"

"Signs in the ... moon"

These are strong symptoms of this era. They indicate that the believer should "look up . . . your redemption draweth nigh."

Demagogues, wrapped in church titles, have enjoyed popularity for a season. *Playing god* is big business, whether on the stage or behind a pulpit. It is also profitable business.

"Beware lest any man spoil you through philosophy and vain deceit, after the tradition of men, after the rudiments of the world, and not after Christ" (Colossians 2:8).

"But there were false prophets also among the people, even as there shall be false teachers among you, who privily shall bring in damnable heresies, even denying the Lord that bought them, and bring upon themselves swift destruction. And many shall follow their pernicious ways; by reason of whom the way of truth shall be evil spoken of" (2 Peter 2:1,2).

"Little children, it is the last time: and as ye have heard that antichrist shall come, even now are there many antichrists; whereby we know that it is the last time" (1 John 2:18).

The play for the "souls of men" (Revelation 18:13) and big merchants (v. 11) handling big merchandise (v. 12) will reach a crescendo as the planet produces from the fruit of its womb, the False Prophet.

One Thing Is Certain

The meeting has been scheduled in the *air*.

It will not be staged at some coliseum, stadium, or plaza.

Pseudo leaders cannot stage their manufactured rallies where Jesus of Nazareth has pledged to meet us. Any "Messiah" or "Saviour" we meet in any other way is a thief and a robber. "Then we which are alive and remain shall be caught up together with them in the clouds, to meet the Lord in the air; and so shall we ever be with the Lord" (1 Thessalonians 4:17).

Dr. Stanley Horton says, "A careless curiosity that does not pay the price of real Bible study and prayer can make a person a good candidate for the devil's deception."

ECOLOGY

The word and the concern have leaped to the forefront in this generation.

Jesus indicated that there would be *celestial* disturbances and *terrestrial* disturbances.

The inanimate and the brute both suffer under the sentence of sin. "For we know that the whole creation groaneth and travaileth in pain together until now" (Romans 8:22).

Man, in industrial greed, has ravished the planet. Man has mismanaged earth as he mismanages his soul, body, mind, and personal affairs. Man rebels at checks and balances. Sin is undisciplined living. It is "wasting his substance with riotous living" (Luke 15:13). The result is always the same "He began to be in want" (v. 14).

Mankind has arrived at this hour.

He has drilled, cut, uncovered, dumped, plowed, crowded, spilled until that which was at hand and plentiful has disappeared.

Scarcity and cost of raw materials feed worldwide inflation.

HOLOCAUST

Fear feeds the markets of psychiatry, welfare, sociology, and the mentally disturbed, and sky rockets the suicide rate.

Isaiah warned a permissive society of impending judgment. "The earth also is defiled under the inhabitants thereof; because they have transgressed the laws. . . . Therefore the inhabitants of the earth are burned, and few men left" (Isaiah 24:5,6).

Society has written new guidelines in sex, marriage, abortion, and capital punishment.

Isaiah warned, "And I will punish the world for its evil . . . and I will cause the arrogancy of the proud to cease, and will lay low the haughtiness of the terrible" (Isaiah 13:11).

Fire—unquenchable flame—is an ogre that haunts the consciousness of mankind every moment. The nuclear powers on this planet possess tools of devastation that make prophecy read like science manuals.

Paul described the period preceding the return of Jesus: "This know also, that in the last days perilous times shall come. For men shall be lovers of their own selves, covetous, boasters, proud, blasphemers, disobedient to parents, unthankful, unholy, without natural affection, trucebreakers, false accusers, incontinent, fierce, despisers of those that are good, traitors, heady, high-minded, lovers of pleasures more than lovers of God; having a form of godliness, but denying the power thereof" (2 Timothy 3:1-5).

Two words say it all, "perilous times." The danger is *shipwreck*.

OUR WORK IS TO PROCLAIM

Jesus did not say the world must be converted.

That did not happen in the angelic host. One third of the host remains in chains.

But the gospel must be *preached*.

"It pleased God by the foolishness of preaching to save them that believe" (1 Corinthians 1:21).

The witness must penetrate every region of darkness. "And hast redeemed us to God by thy blood out of every kindred, and tongue, and people, and nation" (Revelation 5:9).

It isn't in oratory, or sales "technique," or personality. It is being clothed upon. "For the kingdom of

God is not in word, but in power" (1 Corinthians 4:20).

We cannot stop wars, famines, or earthquakes any more than Paul and Silas could keep the Romans from throwing them in prison. But if, like Paul and Silas, we pray and sing praises to God, these calamities can become opportunities to declare the gospel.

They did in the Book of Acts. "And at that time there was great persecution against the church which was at Jerusalem; and they were all scattered abroad throughout the regions of Judea and Samaria, except the apostles" (Acts 8:1).

Just as an airplane moves down the runway against the wind to rise into the sky, so does the church grow and strengthen against opposition. I know this. The gospel has been preached further and farther than ever before. Missionary-evangelism is at its zenith.

THE DAYS OF NOAH

Jesus chose the comparison. What is the significance of:

> "eating and drinking"
> "marrying and giving in marriage"

Perhaps it is a "business-as-usual" attitude. Perhaps it is an emphasis of the flesh. Perhaps it was a philosophy of materialism.

The key words are "and knew not." There was a spiritual and moral numbness. Their own pleasures and plans saturated their lives. There wasn't any room for God. They were *busy*. There was a feeling that it couldn't happen to them.

If the New Testament emphasizes anything, it is the suddenness of Christ's return. A world system makes no allowance for it. "Watch ye therefore: for ye know not when the master of the house cometh, at even, or at midnight, or at the cockcrowing, or in the morning: lest coming suddenly he find you sleeping" (Mark 13:35,36).

It's a tragedy to be dead toward God. "But she that liveth in pleasure is dead while she liveth" (2 Timothy 5:6). That was the condition of Noah's generation. "For to be carnally minded is death" (Romans 8:6).

Their viewpoint was entirely *horizontal*. There was nothing *vertical*. They wanted the sweet-now-and-now and not the sweet-by-and-by. There was no knowledge of God although Noah preached as a witness. "Their foolish heart was darkened" (Romans 1:21).

The comparison is fixed. "So shall also the coming of the Son of man be." The same conditions will prevail.

BETTER BE READY

Vessels without oil can be a tragedy. So many good people will be lost. Jesus describes it. "I know thy works, that thou hast a name that thou livest, and art dead" (Revelation 3:1).

An important word in the promise is the word *alive*. "Then we which are alive and remain shall be caught up" (1 Thessalonians 4:17). There must be spiritual response.

A line of division is established.

Count on it!

"One shall be taken and the other left" (Matthew 24:40).

There is another marker which says, "They that are

Christ's at his coming" (1 Corinthians 15:23). Do you belong to Jesus?

The line is not drawn in the judgment day. It is only revealed then. The choices men make in this life determine on which side they will be.

"Behold, I come as a thief. Blessed is he that watcheth, and keepeth his garments, lest he walk naked, and they see his shame" (Revelation 16:15).

It means something to maintain your testimony for Christ.

WATCH

The big command is to stay alert. The believer is on sentry duty.

It doesn't imply indolence. The directive is to "occupy" your time, your talent, your money, your faith. If we don't, Satan will. We need to crowd him instead of permitting him to crowd us.

Paul lays down these guidelines: "For even when we were with you, this we commanded you, that if any man would not work, neither should he eat. For we hear that there are some which walk among you disorderly, working not at all, but are busybodies. Now them that are such we command and exhort by our Lord Jesus Christ, that with quietness they work, and eat their own bread. But ye, brethren, be not weary in well doing" (2 Thessalonians 3:10-13).

The believer is to exude *optimism*—"look up!" That is a powerful witness when everyone else is looking down. It is better to keep our eyes on Him than on world conditions.

OTHER SIGNS

Other signs to watch are:

The power of capital and management. For reference read James 5:1-8.

The increase of travel and knowledge. For reference read Daniel 12:4.

Apostasy. For reference read Matthew 24:12; 2 Timothy 3:5; 2 Thessalonians 2:3; 2 Peter 3:3,4.

A revival of the occult. For reference read 1 Timothy 4:1-3.

The revival of the nation of Israel. For reference read Jeremiah 30:11; Matthew 24:32-34; Luke 21:24.

The political and military ascendancy of the north. For reference read Ezekiel 39:2.

The revival of the Roman pattern in Europe—a federated state complex. For reference read Daniel 2.

The charismatic renewal. For reference read James 5:7; Acts 3:19.

9 The Gibraltar of Our Faith

The best heaven a sinner ever has is this life. The worst hell a believer ever experiences is here and now.

Paul says the same thing. "Our light affliction, which is but for a moment, worketh for us a far more exceeding and eternal weight of glory" (2 Corinthians 4:17).

It pays to serve Jesus.

The Christian isn't selling a piece of blue sky.

His investment is based upon the pledge of Jesus Christ, "I will come again." There will be eternal dividends. "This same Jesus, which is taken up from you into heaven, shall so come in like manner as ye have seen him go into heaven" (Acts 1:11).

Heaven has big plans for this planet.

It needs *management*—responsible, incorruptible, efficient management. The difference between success and failure is management .We shall reign or *administrate* with Him. This is training time. The believer is tested. He or she is judged in a series of circumstances as to capability and reliability.

The functions of earth, from mail service to maintenance, must have devoted and Christ-oriented personnel to perfect their performances.

It's a big task for a new day.

The Resurrection Is the Guarantee

What Jesus achieved seals my tomorrow.

Without the Resurrection there is no satisfactory explanation for the New Testament. A myth could not support the Acts of the Apostles. The brethren possessed evidence beyond reasonable doubt.

They were scoffers.

They preferred the philosophies of the day. With these they could come to terms with the carnal nature. They could admire and propagate the best out of a world system.

They defined, as sociologists are inclined to define today, immortality to be a projection of genes through children and grandchildren.

Paul rejected their mutterings. Halfway through the first century A.D., false teachers dogged Paul's evangelism. They sought to *modify* Christianity. They wished to make it fit the philosophies held by the intellectuals of their day

Paul scorned their theories.

His language is blunt.

"Fruitless discussion" (1 Timothy 1:6).[1]

"Wanting to be teachers of the Law, even though they do not understand either what they are saying or the matters about which they make confident assertions" (1 Timothy 1:7).

"But have nothing to do with worldly fables fit only for old women" (1 Timothy 4:7).

"Turn away their ears from the truth, and will turn aside to myths" (2 Timothy 4:4).

---

[1]In general, Scripture quotations in the text are from the edition of the King James Version published by the American Bible Society. However, here and occasionally elsewhere in the text the *New American Standard Bible* has been used.

"He is conceited and understands nothing; but he has morbid interest in controversial questions and disputes about words, out of which arise envy, strife, abusive language, evil suspicions, and constant friction between men of depraved mind and deprived of the truth, who suppose that godliness is a means of gain" (1 Timothy 6:4,5).

"Avoiding worldly and empty chatter and the opposing arguments of what is falsely called knowledge" (2 Timothy 2:16).

"Refuse foolish and ignorant speculations, knowing that they produce quarrels" (2 Timothy 2:23).

"Always learning and never able to come to the knowledge of the truth" (2 Timothy 3:7).

This is the language Paul uses to warn Timothy about such meddlers.

PAUL MEETS OBJECTIONS

Paul is always too much for the liberals and modernists.

His polemic for the Resurrection is found in 1 Corinthians 15. He starts with the Jewish Scriptures which taught it.

"For thou wilt not abandon my soul to Sheol; neither wilt Thou allow Thy Holy One to see the pit" (Psalm 16:10).

"He will prolong His days" (Isaiah 53:10).

"He will revive us after two days; He will raise us up on the third day" (Hosea 6:2).

Paul further declares the Resurrection to be *verifiable history*. He lists the physical appearances that Jesus made. There were too many witnesses, and too many circumstances, and too such a crosscut of natures that any possibility of collusion is negative. He

74

ate with them. He taught them. He traveled with them. He made himself known to them.

"He appeared to more than five hundred brethren at one time" (1 Corinthians 15:6).

Paul says that the evidence and the witnesses are there to check. The Resurrection cannot be reduced to an academic debate.

Paul goes further.

He makes the Resurrection the cornerstone of the Christian faith. *Without it the Christian confession crumbles.* "And if Christ has not been raised, your faith is worthless; you are still in your sins" (1 Corinthians 15:17). If there was no future for Him, there is no future for us. My victory is in Him.

I may be happy but I am deluded, "if the dead rise not."

The Resurrection is the Gibraltar of history. It is my guarantee. Because He lives, I live also.

Christ promised His followers that when He returned to the Father He would send the Holy Spirit to them. *One is proof of the other.*

Jesus, who is Prophet, Priest, and King, continues His priestly ministry for us. His intercession is constant. It prevails at all times. "The enemy shall not exact upon him; nor the son of wickedness afflict him. . . . My faithfulness and my mercy shall be with him" (Psalm 89:22,24). I enjoy privileges which the unbeliever does not experience. "Hence, also, He is able to save forever those who draw near to God through Him, since He always lives to make intercession for them" (Hebrews 7:25).

WHEN WILL OUR RESURRECTION OCCUR?

"Christ the firstfruits; afterward they that are Christ's at his coming" (1 Corinthians 15:23).

Christ's at his coming" (1 Corinthians 15:23).

Belonging to Jesus is the only requirement for receiving the full benefits.

There is always an attempt to add something further.

The born-again Methodist, the born-again Lutheran will rise with the born-again Pentecostal.

There is more than rising.

There is glorification.

"And if children, heirs also, heirs of God and fellow-heirs with Christ, if indeed we suffer with Him in order that we may also be glorified with Him" (Romans 8:17).

During this life the human body keeps wasting away, but the believer does not have to waste away with it. The inner man can enjoy constant spiritual renewal.

Paul's life was rugged. Few have equalled it—"imprisonments, beaten times without number, often in danger of death. Five times I received from the Jews thirty-nine lashes. Three times I was beaten with rods, once I was stoned, three times I was shipwrecked, a night and a day I have spent in the deep. I have been on frequent journeys, in dangers from rivers, dangers from robbers, dangers from my countrymen, dangers from the Gentiles, dangers in the city, dangers in the wilderness, dangers on the sea, dangers among false brethren; I have been in labor and hardship, through many sleepless nights, in hunger and thirst, often without food, in cold and exposure" (2 Corinthians 11:23-27).

From that background he told Romans, "I consider that the sufferings of this present time are not worthy to be compared with the glory that is to be revealed to us" (Romans 8:18).

He calls his afflictions light.

The believer's contract is a contract that assures performance. It will take the believer all the way. "Faithful is He who calls you, and He also will bring it to pass" (1 Thessalonians 5:24). "Fixing our eyes on Jesus, the author and perfecter of faith" (Hebrews 12:2).

A New Body

Paul did not groan to be young and strong always.

He did not groan to be repaired or healed.

He groaned for the redemption of the body. "We ourselves groan within ourselves, waiting eagerly for our adoption as sons, the redemption of our body" (Romans 8:23).

Paul was marvelously used in healing. He knew, however, that healings are for the short haul. There await greater privileges. Calvary is the full purchase of this contract.

Sin closed Eden to mankind. Mankind has experienced physical erosion and material opposition. It has been a struggle. Gethsemane and Golgotha opened a way of return.

Calvary isn't *patchwork*. It is *miracle*. "Therefore if any man is in Christ, he is a new creature; the old things passed away; behold, new things have come" (2 Corinthians 5:17).

We are a "new creature" in an old environment. We are like the deepsea diver. We are dependent upon a saving element. There must be a connection from below to above.

Presently there will be a new environment. Then

the situation will change. A new heaven and a new earth will support a new body.

What happened to Jesus was different from what happened to Lazarus. Christ moved through the wrappings. Lazarus had to be unbound.

WHAT KIND OF BODY?

It will be "fashioned"—*designed* like Christ's present body. "Who will transform the body of our humble state into conformity with the body of His glory, by the exertion of the power that He has even to subject all things to himself" (Philippians 3:21). John promises, "We shall be like Him" (1 John 3:2).

The new body will be *immortal* and *incorruptible*. It will not be subject to sin, decay, or death.

It will be a *real body*. There will be identity and personality. But it will be spiritual, not natural or earthy. It is adjusted to heaven and not to hell. It fits the inner man. It feeds on affection for Christ and not on appetite for a world system. "If there is a natural body, there is also a spiritual body. . . . However, the spiritual is not first, but the natural; then the spiritual" (1 Corinthians 15:44-46).

By spiritual the Bible does not mean *ghostly*. Heaven isn't Halloween.

Physical limitations will be removed. Mental, emotional, social, worship capacities will be enlarged. I can achieve the man I want to be in Christ. I can sing, I can write, I can think, I can speak as I should, without embarrassment, to the glory of God. I will no longer experience weariness, loss of memory, failure to interpret, pain, inability to comprehend. *The new body will be a perfect instrument.*

We see a preview in Jesus.

He could enter and leave through locked doors. He was at home in either matter or space. Yet He invited a complete physical examination. "Reach here your finger, and see My hands; and reach here your hand, and put it into My side" (John 20:27).

He convinced the most skeptical among His friends that He was the same Jesus.

GETTING READY

This new body is not for now.

What happens when I am buried? Am I "unclothed?" Am I spirit only? One thing is certain. I am in the presence of the Lord. "For we walk by faith, not by sight—we are of good courage, I say, and prefer rather to be absent from the body and to be at home with the Lord" (2 Corinthians 5:7,8).

The Holy Spirit is commissioned to accomplish far more in the believer than to give him boldness and assurance in testimony. The Holy Spirit is faithfully transforming the believer—getting that believer ready for his or her presentation. It starts at conversion. There is so much to be done. Peter sensed what was happening within himself. He was *growing*. He was maturing. "For if these qualities are yours and are increasing, they render you neither useless nor unfruitful in the true knowledge of our Lord Jesus Christ" (2 Peter 1:8).

In God's moment a spirit made ready will be clothed upon.

"And raised us up with Him, and seated us with Him in the heavenly places, in Christ Jesus" (Ephesias 2:6). Paul says that kind of living is ad infinitum: "And so shall we ever be with the Lord" (1 Thessalonians 4:17).

There will be a payday on earth. There will be a payday in heaven. What I have earned, or what I have forfeited, will be realized.

Christ holds His servants *accountable*.

"For we shall stand before the judgment seat of God" (Romans 14:10).

"And I say to you, that every careless word that men shall speak, they shall render account for in the day of judgment. For by your words you shall be justified, and by your words you shall be condemned" (Matthew 12:36,37).

"For the Son of Man is going to come in the glory of His Father with His angels: and will then recompense every man according to his deeds" (Matthew 16:27).

"And you will be blessed, since they do not have the means to repay you; for you will be repaid at the resurrection of the righteous" (Luke 14:14).

"Therefore do not go on passing judgment before the time, but wait until the Lord comes who will both bring to light the things hidden in the darkness and disclose the motives of men's hearts; and then each man's praise will come to him from God" (1 Corinthians 4:5).

"Behold, I am coming quickly, and My reward is with Me, to render to every man according to what he has done" (Revelation 22:12).

Privileges bring responsibility.

The greater privilege brings the greater responsibility.

Responsibility means accounting.

Accounts will be rendered and balanced.

Some will be *ashamed*. Others will be *confident*.

"And now, little children, abide in Him, so that when He appears, we may have confidence and not shrink away from Him in shame at His coming" (1 John 2:28).

Premium is placed upon faithfulness.

"For bodily discipline is only of little profit, but godliness is profitable for all things, since it holds promise for the present life and also for the life to come" (1 Timothy 4:8).

"You were faithful with a few things, I will put you in charge of many things, enter into the joy of your master" (Matthew 25:21).

I shall be judged for *motive*.

Some records will be as worthless as hay, stubble, and kindling. Others will endure like gold, silver, and as precious stones. "Rejoice, and be glad, for your reward in heaven is great" (Matthew 5:12).

Jesus warned!

"Beware of practicing your righteousness before men to be noticed by them; otherwise you have no reward with your father who is in heaven" (Matthew 6:1).

Even *details* are judged. "For whoever gives you a cup of water to drink because of your name as followers of Christ, truly I say to you, he shall not lose his reward" (Mark 9:41).

INCENTIVES

The knowledge that my service will be weighed should make me careful. I want what I do to have His approval—"Well done."

I should never kill time. I am a steward. I must make time count.

Paul felt that way. "Woe is unto me, if I preach not

the gospel" (1 Corinthians 9:16). He felt he was a "debtor"—that he owed something for his great release in Christ. He believed that in this life only there was opportunity to be saved. "Therefore knowing the fear of the Lord, we persuade men, but we are made manifest to God; and I hope that we are made manifest also in your consciences" (2 Corinthians 5:11).

Then Christ will not deal with *personal* sins. Long since they are under the Blood. He will judge the believer's *service*. How much has been selfish? How much has been unworthy?

Yes, there will be screening!

Rebelliousness, unfaithfulness bring exclusion. Such will not stand with the company of God on the other side. "For this you know with certainty, that no immoral or impure person or covetous man, who is an idolator, has an inheritance in the kingdom of Christ and God" (Ephesians 5:5). "Or do you not know that the unrighteous shall not inherit the kingdom of God? Do not be deceived; neither fornicators, nor idolators, nor adulterers, nor effeminate, nor homosexuals, nor thieves, nor the covetous, nor drunkards, nor revilers, nor swindlers, shall inherit the kingdom of God" (1 Corinthians 6:9,10).

Again!

Those who receive the grace of God but fail to let it operate in their lives will also be barred from heaven. The grace we receive must flow out to others or we lose it.

"So shall My heavenly Father also do to you, if each of you does not forgive his brother from your heart" (Matthew 18:35).

Eternity will mark and notice examples of the gospel on earth. "And when the Chief Shepherd appears, you will receive the unfading crown of glory" (1 Peter 5:4).

This present body is a servant. It is Mr. Outward Man meant to be obedient to Mr. Inward Man. Since its duration is determined—from the cradle to the coffin—it has affection for things below. Thus it lusts against Mr. Inward Man. It cannot be reconciled. It must be brought into subjection, into service. Otherwise living will be upside down. You will be miserable and out-of-step inside.

When we stimulate the Inward Man to set his affection upon things above, there is a sweetness, a reasonableness that possesses us. It is the assurance that we are moving toward *completeness*—that the new body will fit the "new man."

My assurance stems from the ministry of the Holy Spirit within me as Chairman of my life. He is shaping me for things to come. I know that as I yield, my reward is certain. That is His witness to me.

10 The Great Shoot-out

There will be *confrontation*.

It is evident that an antichrist spirit is already working in the world. This spirit will find incarnation in one man. "And then shall that Wicked be revealed, whom the Lord shall consume with the spirit of his mouth, and shall destroy with the brightness of his coming" (2 Thessalonians 2:8).

Speculation is always an intriguing practice, but it is not a safe one. It has produced many false prophets and errant interpretations; it will continue to do so. These lead people astray.

Stay with what the Bible says!

Jumping to conclusions is the world's favorite exercise.

Christ sent the Holy Spirit to be Teacher. He guides into all truth. The Bible is truth. The Holy Spirit will direct us to the Word and in the Word.

He is not responsible for theories that come from lazy driftings of human imagination.

CONFUSION

The Thessalonians were confused.

They misunderstood the plan and the purpose of Christ's return. Paul wrote letters to them to correct this misunderstanding.

He told them in no uncertain terms that Jesus had not yet returned. Neither the Great Tribulation nor the Millennium had begun. Paul states a sequence of events that precede these eras.

A *great apostasy* will precede Christ's return.

"That day shall not come, except there come a falling away first" (2 Thessalonians 2:3).

That man of sin shall be *revealed.* The reference is to Antichrist. "And that man of sin be revealed, the son of perdition" (2 Thessalonians 2:3).

The believer will have his man. The unbeliever will have his man. The believer will enjoy a parenthesis of "supper." The unbeliever will endure a period of suffering.

Jesus, on one occasion, said to His countrymen, "And ye yourselves like unto men that wait for their Lord, when he will return from the wedding" (Luke 12:36). The believer is oriented to the wedding.

As surely as the unbeliever will be present for the revealing of his choice—"that man of sin"—so shall the believer be present for the revealing of his choice— the Bridegroom.

The believer is not confused about the man. The believer is identified with Jesus of Nazareth—not "the son of perdition."

The new birth is not an envelope of segregation. Christians do suffer. They are involved. History makes that plain. They suffer for Christ's sake.

The wrath of God is manifest during the Tribulation. Christ bore that "wrath" at Calvary. "He that heareth my word, and believeth on him that sent me, hath everlasting life, and shall not come into condemnation; but is passed from death unto life" (John 5:24). The case of the believer is settled out of court.

"Shall not come into condemnation" is the contract. Condemnation action will not be instituted against him.

"Pour out the vials of the wrath of God upon the earth" (Revelation 16:1).

The believer doesn't need a "Protestant purgatory."

Calvary is *sufficient*. The only plus sign any sinner, saved by the grace of God, needs is that middle cross. That says it all.

No Repentance

When the trumpets bring a series of partial judgments, the Bible states that a third of mankind was killed, and those who were not killed "repented not" (Revelation 9:18,20). Forgiveness and cleansing are predicated upon confession and repentance. Read Psalm 51!

When further judgments follow, it is stated three times that mankind repented not (Revelation 16:9, 11,21).

Righteous people may become objects of God's *chastening*. Such is loving discipline administered by a parent to a child. The Revelation does not describe such chastening. It describes "the *wrath* of God." The believer is never the object of his Father's wrath. Don't confuse God with the devil! "God hath not appointed us to wrath, but to obtain salvation by our Lord Jesus Christ" (1 Thessalonians 5:9).

A Short Period

A figure of three and one-half is mentioned in the Old and New Testaments.

It will be the *showdown*.

God announces Christ *victor*.

Daniel describes it: "But the judgment shall sit, and they shall take away his dominion, to consume and to destroy. . . . And the kingdom and dominion, *and the greatness of the kingdom under the whole heaven,* shall be given to the people of the saints of the Most High, whose kingdom is an everlasting kingdom, and all dominions shall serve and obey him" (Daniel 7:26,27).

John describes it. Antichrist's sway is limited. "And there was given unto him a mouth speaking great things and blasphemies; and power was given unto him to continue forty and two months" (Revelation 13:5).

Antichrist's manifestation and evangelism will comfortably compare, in length, to our Lord's little more than three years of public ministry.

Man's choice will have his opportunity. Then he will meet heaven's objection as God's choice met hell's objection.

The lawless one will *demand* worship.

"He shall speak great words against the Most High" (Daniel 7:25). "Who opposeth and exalteth himself above all that is called God, or that is worshipped; so that he as God sitteth in the temple of God, showing himself that he is God" (2 Thessalonians 2:4).

Christ made no demands. His is *invitation.* "Come unto me, all ye that labor and are heavy laden, and I will give you rest. Take my yoke upon you, and learn of me; for I am meek and lowly in heart: and ye shall find rest unto your souls. For my yoke is easy, and my burden is light" (Matthew 11:28-30).

One is the man *of* sin; the other is the Man for sin. "God sending his own Son in the likenes of sinful flesh, and for sin, condemned sin the flesh" (Romans

87

8:3). Paul tells us, "God commendeth His love toward us, in that, while we were yet sinners, Christ died for us" (Romans 5:8).

It is still Christ or Barabbas.

Choice means destiny.

THE BRIDEGROOM COMETH

The believer's expectancy is warranted. "And when these things begin to come to pass, then look up, and lift up your heads; for your redemption draweth nigh" (Luke 21:28).

There is an unmistakable admonition for the believer: "Watch ye therefore, and pray always, that ye may be accounted worthy to escape all these things that shall come to pass, and to stand before the Son of Man" (Luke 21:36).

There is a promise made by the Bridegroom to the Bride: "Because thou hast kept the word of my patience, I also will keep thee from the hour of temptation, which shall come upon all the world, to try them that dwell upon the earth" (Revelation 3:10).

HINDRANCE

Jesus called the believer "salt" and "light." They are effective deterrents to corruption and darkness.

Paul speaks of the Vicar of Christ upon earth—the Holy Spirit. "He who now [hindreth] will [hinder], until he be taken out of the way" (2 Thessalonians 2:7).

The present ministry of the Holy Spirit is to reveal the Father and the Son—the perfect, redeeming relationship toward mankind. "He shall glorify me; for he shall receive of mine, and shall show it unto you. All things that the Father hath are mine: therefore said I, that he shall take of mine, and shall show it unto you" (John 16:14,15).

The lawless spirit of the day is *an alarm,* warning loudly that the presence of the Holy Spirit—that presence resident upon earth—will abruptly terminate.

God has always exercised, imposed *restraint.* The Book of Job is an example. It is awesome to contemplate a planet where all divine restraint is lifted.

We are at present flirting with *flood signs.*

"But as the days of Noah were, so shall also the coming of the Son of man be. For as in the days that were before the flood they were eating and drinking, marrying and giving in marriage, until the day that Noah entered into the ark, and knew not until the flood came, *and took them all away*" (Matthew 24: 37-39).

There is a point of no return.

As surely as Lot was removed from Sodom and Noah was removed from his generation, a witness will be removed, and then wrath will be manifest.

Furthermore, Israel has a date with Antichrist. The "restrainers" are God's people, for the most part in the Western nations, who influence their governments, in foreign policy, toward Israel. This action must change before Israel is brought to judgment for her cumulative and repetitive sins. "Who both killed the Lord Jesus, and their own prophets, and have persecuted us; and they please not God, and are contrary to all men: . . . to fill up their sins always: for the wrath is come upon them to the uttermost" (1 Thessalonians 2:15,16).

ANTICHRIST

Antichrist will come from the pit. "The beast that

ascendeth out of the bottomless pit" (Revelation 11:7). He is Satan's representative. He will be fashioned by hell.

A well-known proposition in geopolitics states that he who ruleth Europe ruleth the world, and he that ruleth Germany ruleth Europe. That pattern remains a strong silhouette since the crumbling of the Roman-Caesar design with the passing of Charlemagne.

Both the idealists, like Ramsay MacDonald and Woodrow Wilson, and the realists, like Napoleon and Hitler, have believed that the destiny of earth and mankind rest upon the restoration of the Roman pattern—a United States of Europe. *That outline is always visible.*

There is also a pattern of segments of Europe always willing to follow the leader. Italy is an example. In World War I it tumbled toward the Allies. In World War II it fell in with Hitler. The Strong Man on the horizon will gain control of three of these segments. Quickly seven others will delegate powers to him. He will be accepted as a political genius. "In this horn [seat of authority] were eyes like the eyes of man, and a mouth speaking great things" (Daniel 7:8). Daniel gives some idea of sweeping changes he institutes. "And think to change times and laws" (Daniel 7:25).

He will brilliantly tackle economic snafus. "And through his policy also he shall cause craft to prosper in his hand" (Daniel 8:25). He will institute a police state and abrogate all electives of management and labor. "And he causeth all, both small and great, rich and poor, free and bond, to receive a mark in their right hand, or in their foreheads: and that no man might buy or sell, save he that had the mark, or the name of the beast, or the number of his name" (Revelation 13:16,17).

He will supplant all religion with his own, directed by his personal high priest, the False Prophet. He will attempt to erase every vestige of Christianity. "And his power shall be mighty . . . and he shall destroy wonderfully, and shall prosper, and practise, and shall destroy the mighty and the holy people" (Daniel 8:24). John says he will ravage earth. "And cause that as many as would not worship the image of the beast should be killed" (Revelation 13:15).

Knowing that man must have a religion of some kind, he will establish one based on the divinity of man and the supremacy of the state.

THE TRAP

At first, the Antichrist will seem tolerant of the Jews.

He will make a covenant with them.

This will be Israel's final folly.

Israel passionately desires a worldwide acceptance of her sovereignty, her right to be a nation. Her contract, as the believer's is, and her security, as the believer's is, is in the Word of God—not in the acceptance of the nations around her, nor, in the believer's case, the acceptance by a world system.

Antichrist will offer Israel "a covenant." "And he shall confirm the covenant with many for one week [one period of seven years]: and in the midst of the week he shall cause the sacrifice and the oblation to cease, and for the overspreading of abominations he shall make it desolate, even until the consummation" (Daniel 9:27).

Jesus warned His countrymen that it would happen.

"I am come in my Father's name, and ye receive me not: if another shall come in his own name, him ye will receive" (John 5:43).

One more time Israel will cry, "We have no king but Caesar." And one more time a false sense of security will pull the roof down over their heads.

It is during this brief period of calm that Israel restores her great, national symbol, the temple. The deceptive plans of the Antichrist are for the temple to be rebuilt at Israel's expense, then quickly use it as a vehicle for a worldwide public relations program of imagery. "So that he as God sitteth in the temple of God, showing himself that he is God" (2 Thessalonians 2:4).

"JACOB'S TROUBLE"

This perfidy and misery are emphasized by many prophets. "Alas! for that day is great, so that none is like it: it is even the time of Jacob's trouble; but he shall be saved out of it" (Jeremiah 30:7). Jesus described it. "For then shall be great tribulation, such as was not since the beginning of the world to this time, no, nor ever shall be" (Matthew 24:21).

With the believers evacuated, Antichrist will seek Israel's demise. He, too, like Eichman, Himmler, and predecessors, like Haman and Pharaoh, will seek "the final solution" to mankind's most knotty problem.

Daniel, the greatest statesman of all time, saw it. "There shall be a time of trouble, such as never was since there was a nation even to that same time" (Daniel 12:1).

Antichrist's determination will be to make Israel accept him as God. This will be the blasphemy of blasphemies. "He shall exalt himself, and magnify himself above every god, and shall speak marvelous things against the God of gods" (Daniel 11:36).

Israel's resistance is described by the prophets. "The city [Jerusalem] shall be taken, and the houses rifled, and the women ravished" (Zechariah 14:2).

THE DECEIVER

Antichrist, too, will evangelize "with signs following." Paul calls them "lying wonders" and "with all deceivableness of unrighteousness" (2 Thessalonians 2:10).

He will bind "the souls of men" (Revelation 18: 13) by *lies*. His trademark from hell will be Satan's imprint—a liar and a murderer. Deceit must have suitable soil to prosper. Such soil is in evidence. "Because they received not the love of the truth . . . but had pleasure in unrighteousness (2 Thessalonians 2: 10,12). That is the New Testament indictment. Jesus said, "And this is the condemnation, that light is come into the world, and men loved darkness rather than light, because their deeds were evil" (John 3:19).

Nothing robs and punishes like a lie.

Rejection brings judgment. "And for this cause God shall send them strong delusion, that they should believe a lie: that they all might be damned who believed not the truth, but had pleasure in unrighteousness" (2 Thessalonians 2:11,12).

Paul warned the Romans of his day that the same thing had happened to past generations. "For the wrath of God is revealed from heaven against all ungodliness and unrighteousness of men who hold the truth in unrighteousness" (Romans 1:18).

He says again, "Wherefore God also gave them up to uncleanness, through the lusts of their own hearts

. . . who changed the truth of God into a lie, and worshipped and served the creature more than the Creator" (Romans 1:24,25).

It is a planet abandoned by "the Spirit of Truth," wallowing helplessly under the dictation of the Deceiver.

Antichrist promises to lead mankind to peace and prosperity. It is an age-old political promise.

His tools are militant—war, conquest, rigidity, death.

It will be a night of terror before the dawning of the glad millennial day. "Watchman, what of the night? The watchman said, The morning cometh, and also the night" (Isaiah 21:11,12).

It will be the Great Purge as well as the Great Tribulation.

This is the story that the major chapters of the Revelation document—the Judgments. The prayers of God's heritage have been "Thy kingdom come." It will. John sees "much incense" added to these prayers. That means such prayers have been accepted and will be answered. "And the smoke of the incense, which came with the prayers of the saints, ascended up before God out of the angel's hand" (Revelation 8:4).

JUDGMENTS

The fraction, *one-third,* is repeated.

A third part of the sea is turned to blood. A third part of shipping is destroyed. A third part of the sun, moon, and stars are darkened.

Demons are loosed upon the earth.

Militant hordes from "the East" move westward to smother western culture and standards of living. They bring death to a third of mankind.

Plagues, reminiscent of those judging Pharaoh and Egypt, visit earth. The sun scorches. Water is polluted. Earth is covered with stygian darkness. Mountains are leveled. Islands disappear. Hail, weighing 62 pounds a hailstone, bombards mankind.

The series and the schedule of judgments are detailed in the Revelation.

ARMAGEDDON

Antichrist, with his "mouth," the False Prophet, will speak satanically. They will persuade political leaders that a United Nations' effort should be made to eliminate the last marks of any God-consciousness upon earth. This will be the last of the Crusades—a crusade in reverse—a total world effort to eliminate God. They will choose Israel for a battleground. God will meet them in the historic Valley of Jezreel, near the site of Megiddo. It is also known as the Plain of Esdraelon. The battle line will probably extend far to the south, past the plains of Jericho to Bozrah (Petra) in the Sinai, southeast of the Dead Sea.

Armageddon is "the shoot-out" of a Christ-denying world system against the sovereignty of God. It is the final high-water mark of a world system—"the mystery of ungodliness."

Suddenly, Christ will appear in power and great glory. That story is told in Revelation 19:11-15.

Jesus will bring His heavenly army. We are given glimpses of that army in the Scriptures. "Behold, the Lord cometh with ten thousands of his saints" (Jude 14). "The Lord my God shall come, and all the saints with thee" (Zechariah 14:5). "The chariots of God are twenty thousand, even thousands of angels: the Lord is among them" (Psalm 68:17).

David, a military genius in his own right, sees prophetically the outcome of the battle: "Why do the nations rage, and the people imagine a vain thing? The kings of the earth set themselves, and the rulers take counsel together, against the Lord, and against his Anointed, saying, "Let us break their bands asunder, and cast away their cords from us. He that sitteth in the heavens shall laugh: the Lord shall have them in derision" (Psalm 2:1-4).

Before the battle is fought God will summon vultures to feast upon the carnage. "Saying to all the fowls that fly in the midst of heaven, "Come and gather yourselves together unto the supper of the great God; that ye may eat the flesh of kings, and the flesh of captains, and the flesh of mighty men, and the flesh of horses, and of them that sit on them, and the flesh of all men, both free and bond, both small and great" (Revelation 19:17,18). The story is also told in Ezekiel 39:4,11-22.

Jesus will speak the word and *five-sixths* of the adversary forces will die. "And leave but the sixth part of thee" (Ezekiel 39:2).

Burial details will work for *seven months*.

The salvage will supply Israel fuel for *seven years*.

Antichrist and the False Prophets will be *cast alive* into the lake of fire.

11 Utopia at Last

Millennium!

The word even sounds good and looks good and feels good.

And it is. It is the promise of better things.

Politicians have always made such promises. But God is not a politician.

A figure has been set. It is a figure of 1,000 years. The phrase is repeated in the twentieth chapter of the Book of Revelation. "And he laid hold on the dragon, that old serpent, which is the Devil, and Satan, and bound him a thousand years" (Revelation 20:2).

You support a loser when you serve the devil.

One thing is certain. There can be no peace on earth as long as Satan is rampant. Men plan millenniums. They cannot produce them. Evil must be bound and only God can bind it.

This happens at Armageddon. Jesus is Victor. Calvary is too much for Satan. "And Jesus answered them, saying, The hour is come, that the Son of Man should be glorified" (John 12:23). "Now is the judgment of this world: now shall the prince of this world be cast out" (John 12:31).

Satan is already under *indictment*. His *sentence* will begin at Armageddon.

The beginning of the arrest action is described by John. "There was war in heaven: Michael and his angels fought against the dragon; and the dragon fought and his angels, and prevailed not; neither was their place found any more in heaven. And the great dragon was cast out, that old serpent, called the Devil, and Satan, which deceiveth the whole world: he was cast out into the earth, and his angels were cast out with him" (Revelation 12:7-9).

Satan is *falling*. The believer is *climbing*.

Satan's antagonism is based on this. He is heading toward the judgment our sin-destiny would sentence us. The redeemed are moving toward the favor and privilege Satan once enjoyed and forfeited through pride.

FREED FROM DECEIT

That will be glorious freedom.

Only then can the New Deal, the Great Society, the New World Order, the Fair Deal be realized. Daniel visualized it. "The God of heaven [shall] set up a kingdom, which shall never be destroyed" (Daniel 2:44). He says that every vestige of the old order fostered and supported by a world system, under obedience to Satan, will be crushed and disappear.

There will be *a new order*.

The change in government and society and economy will be as complete as the structure change in animals. Nothing will remain of cherished tradition and social and economic dogma. Christ will not be advised by psychiatrists and economists. They have tangled and confused mankind sufficiently. Truth will be applied, and will prevail, in the very sinews of society.

What a cleansing!

Our culture is cluttered by Babylonian astrology, Medo-Persian ethics, Greek philosophy, and Roman law. We are a potpourri of ideas, hyperboles, and wishful thinking. They have built on each other until a jungle of fears and fancies submerge the public. The "image" needs to be hit, and hit hard. Daniel says it will be. He says it "became like the chaff of the summer threshingfloors; and the wind carried them away, that no place was found for them" (Daniel 2: 35).

"The government shall be upon his shoulder" (Isaiah 9:6). Christ will take full responsibility for earth. This planet needs new management.

WHO WILL BE INVOLVED?

Two classes will be involved. There will be those who reign with Christ. There will be those governed.

"The kingdoms of this world are become the kingdoms of our Lord" (Revelation 11:15). The "kingdoms of this world" are the great empires of commerce and the powers of political parties. They are the unions, and interlocking banking muscle, and intrenched sovereigns of utilities. They are the regents of transportation and communication. They dictate mankind's subsistence and pleasure.

Their weaknesses are public knowledge. Mail service grows more costly and deteriorates. Energy needs furnish more and more squabble and higher prices.

Taxes rise and property owners stagger under heavier loads. Violence and lust run the show. Greed and treachery undermine public service. A "new seed" —tried and trained in holiness and absolute commitment to Christ—is needed to *administrate* everything from postal departments to courts.

The believer is coming back. This is his habitat. With full redemptive assets, and relieved from humiliating influences of his old body-vehicle, the believer will accomplish on earth what God intended man to accomplish originally—manage this planet under God. "Subdue it: and have dominion" (Genesis 1:28).

Our place is *with* the Lord. "And so shall we ever be with the Lord" (1 Thessalonians 4:17).

WHAT ABOUT ISRAEL?

Israel also will have a new start. "I make all things new" (Revelation 21:5).

"Behold, the days come, saith the Lord, that I will make a new covenant with the house of Israel, and with the house of Judah" (Jeremiah 31:31).

It is in the blueprint.

"A new heart also will I give you, and a new spirit will I put within you: and I will take away the stony heart out of your flesh, and I will give you an heart of flesh. And I will put my Spirit within you, and cause you to walk in my statutes, and ye shall keep my judgments, and do them" (Ezekiel 36:26,27).

How will this be done?

It will be accomplished through Spirit-filled and Spirit-led residue of the most hated people of human record. One hundred forty-four thousand are *sealed*. Paul defines the sealing of the new covenant. "In whom ye also trusted, after that ye heard the word of truth, the gospel of your salvation: in whom also, after that ye believed, ye were sealed with that Holy Spirit of promise" (Ephesians 1:13). God works in Israel the same way He has worked in the believer.

God has no substitute for the baptism in the Holy Spirit.

"He shall baptize you with the Holy Ghost, and with fire" (Matthew 3:11). God will do for the residue of Israel what He has done for the ecclesia among the nations.

Among the brought back—the resurrected—will be:

1. Believers to govern with Jesus
2. The martyred during the Tribulation
3. The new seed of Israel

The wicked dead will not be resurrected until 1,000 years have passed.

A fragment of earth's population survives the terrors of Antichrist and the retribution of heaven. The great rebuilding and refurbishing of a planet, finally freed from the Usurper, will employ the trusted services of believer, martyr, and Israeli. That is a better coalition than any group a world system has ever put together.

Under Jesus they will extend *the new order* into every realm of living. The changes will fulfill the utopia hoped for since man's expulsion from Eden.

CHANGES

There will be *physical* changes.

The Flood caused topographical changes. "All the fountains of the great deep [were] broken up, and the windows of heaven were opened" (Genesis 7:11). Think what weight, erosion, current did!

Changes are scheduled at Christ's return to this planet.

When His feet touch Olivet, the elevation will divide. One part will move northward, the other southward. This will produce a great, new valley in Israel. "And his feet shall stand in that day upon the mount of Olives, which is before Jerusalem on the east, and the mount of Olives shall cleave in the midst thereof toward the east and toward the west, and there shall be a very great valley; and half of the mountain shall remove toward the north, and half of it toward the south" (Zechariah 14:4).

Much of Israel will be reshaped.

"For, behold, the Lord cometh forth out of his place, and will come down, and tread upon the high places of the earth. And the mountains shall be molten under him, and the valleys shall be cleft, as wax before the fire" (Micah 1:3,4). A large plain will be formed near Jerusalem. "All the land shall be turned as a plain from Geba to Rimmon south of Jerusalem" (Zechariah 14:10).

There will be changes in Jerusalem.

These are described by Ezekiel in the latter chapters of his prophecy, beginning with chapter 40. The final temple will be located about 15 miles north of Jerusalem. It will be a new location for a new era. "Nevertheless we, according to his promise, look for new heavens and a new earth, wherein dwelleth righteousness" (2 Peter 3:13). Old associations are broken.

From this temple a river will flow southward to Jerusalem. "A fountain shall come forth of the house of the Lord, and shall water the valley of Shittim [Acacias—in the former wilderness area west of the Jordan]" (Joel 3:18). At Jerusalem, the river will flow into the great valley formed by the fracture of the Mount of Olives and divide into two branches. One branch will flow west into the Mediterranean. The other branch will flow east through the valley to the Dead Sea and on out into the Read Sea. "And it shall be in that day, that living waters shall go out from Jerusalem; half of them toward the former sea, and half of them toward the hinder sea: in summer and in winter shall it be" (Zechariah 14:8).

What a contrast to the present where every drop of water is husbanded in Jerusalem and placed under strict government authority!

This will bring life to the Dead Sea area. There will be supernatural production "because their waters they issued out of the *sanctuary*" (Ezekiel 47:12). The complete story is told in Ezekiel 47:8-12.

ECONOMIC UPHEAVALS

Greed will be eliminated—the virus that exploits distribution, profit, production, management, research, and earth's stockpile.

"The meek shall inherit the earth; and shall delight themselves in the abundance of peace" (Psalm 37:11).

The ecologist will realize his dream. The planet will be restored to fertility and prosperity. "The desert shall rejoice, and blossom as the rose . . . for in the wilderness shall waters break out, and streams in the desert" (Isaiah 35:1,6). Isaiah gives details. "Instead of the thorn shall come up the fir tree, and instead of the brier shall come up the myrtle tree" (Isaiah 55:13).

Amos agrees.

"Behold, the days come, saith the Lord, that the plowman shall overtake the reaper, and the treader of grapes him that soweth seed; and the mountains shall drop sweet wine, and all the hills shall melt" (Amos 9:13).

"For we know that the whole creation groaneth and travaileth in pain . . . *waiting*" (Romans 8:22,23).

There will be *justice*.

"With righteousness shall he judge the poor, and reprove with equity for the meek of the earth" (Isaiah 11:4). No longer will influence and money tip the scales. "He shall judge the poor of the people, he shall save the children of the needy" (Psalms 72:4).

Huge defense budgets and armament races will be erased.

"And he shall judge among many people, and rebuke strong nations afar off; and they shall beat their swords into plowshares, and their spears into pruning hooks; nation shall not lift up a sword against nation, neither shall they learn war any more. But they shall sit every man under his vine and under his fig tree; and none shall make them afraid: for the mouth of the Lord of hosts hath spoken it" (Micah 4:3,4; see Isaiah 2:4; Joel 3:10; Psalm 72:7).

It will be Paradise regained.

ANIMALS WILL BE CHANGED TOO

The mood of tranquility will bring changes in the animal kingdom. "The wolf also shall dwell with the lamb, and the leopard shall lie down with the kid; and the calf and the young lion and the fatling together; and a little child shall lead them. And the cow and the bear shall feed; their young ones shall lie down together; and the lion shall eat straw like the ox. . . . They shall not hurt nor destroy in all my holy mountain" (Isaiah 11:6,7,9).

A NEW WORLD CAPITAL

The city, where the Only Begotten Son of God paid

redemption's price, will become the capital city of the world.

"For the nation and kingdom that will not serve thee shall perish; yea, those nations shall be utterly wasted. . . . The sons also of them that afflicted thee shall come bending unto thee; and all they that despised thee shall bow themselves down at the soles of thy feet; and they shall call thee, The city of the Lord, The Zion of the Holy One of Israel" (Isaiah 60:12,14).

Jewish temperament will change.

"I will pour upon the house of David, and upon the inhabitants of Jerusalem, the spirit of grace and supplications" (Zechariah 12:10).

The Shekinah glory that hovered over tabernacle and temple will return. It will signify God's literal presence.

"And, behold, the glory of the God of Israel came from the way of the east: and his voice was like a noise of many waters: and the earth shined with his glory. And it was according to the appearance of the vision which I saw, even according to the vision that I saw when I came to destroy the city: and the visions were like the vision that I saw by the river Chebar; and I fell upon my face. And the glory of the Lord came into the house by the way of the gate whose prospect is toward the east. So the Spirit took me up, and brought me into the inner court; and, behold, the glory of the Lord filled the house" (Ezekiel 43: 2-5).

"When the Lord shall have washed away the filth of the daughters of Zion, and shall have purged the blood of Jerusalem from the midst thereof by the spirit of judgment, and by the spirit of burning. And the Lord will create upon every dwelling place of mount Zion, and upon her assemblies, a cloud and smoke by day, and the shining of a flaming fire by night: for upon all the glory shall be a defense. And there shall be a tabernacle for a shadow in the daytime from the heat, and for a place of refuge, and for a covert from storm and from rain" (Isaiah 4:4-6).

There will be *a full revelation.* Earth will know God. "The earth shall be full of the knowledge of the Lord, as the waters cover the sea" (Isaiah 11:9). "And they shall teach no more every man his neighbor, and every man his brother, saying, Know the Lord: for they shall all know me, from the least of them unto the greatest of them" (Jeremiah 31:34).

Reverence, respect, religious fervor will be universal.

It will be a different order of things.

Today's allurements—mental trifles and sensual tidbits—will abdicate. God's glory will submerge them.

It will be a return to Eden. "But as truly as I live, all the earth shall be filled with the glory of the Lord" (Numbers 14:21).

The promise has been on the books for a long time.

It will be an old-fashioned camp meeting atmosphere. "And many people shall go and say, Come ye, and let us go up to the mountain of the Lord, to the house of the God of Jacob; and he will teach us of his ways, and we will walk in his paths: for out of Zion shall go forth the law, and the word of the Lord from Jerusalem" (Isaiah 2:3).

A hunger for *teaching* will be satisfied. There is hunger and a thirst in mankind for righteousness. It will be expressed and satisfied. "For, from the rising of the sun even unto the going down of the same, my name shall be great among the Gentiles; and in every place incense shall be offered unto my name, and a pure offering: for my name shall be great among the heathen, saith the Lord of hosts" (Malachi 1:11).

DECISION MAKING

The redeemed with Christ will exercise judgment upon earth. The executive action of God's people, reigning with Christ, will be final. There will be no course of appeal. "Do you not know that the saints shall judge the world? and if the world shall be judged by you, are ye unworthy to judge the smallest matters? Know ye not that we shall judge angels? *how much more things that pertain to this life*" (1 Corinthians 6:2,3).

Corruption, opposition, merchandising sin will not be permitted. "He shall smite the earth with the rod of his mouth, and with the breath of his lips shall he slay the wicked" (Isaiah 11:4).

A CHANGE IN LIFE SPAN

Life will lengthen under millennial conditions.

"There shall be no more thence an infant of days, nor an old man that hath not filled his days: for the child shall die a hundred years old; but the sinner being a hundred years old shall be accursed. . . . They shall not build, and another inhabit; they shall not plant, and another eat: for as the days of a tree are the days of my people, and mine elect shall long enjoy the work of their hands" (Isaiah 65:20,22).

The funeral business will be the poorest business on earth. And it will be hard to sell cemetery plots and tombstones. "Moreover the light of the moon shall be as the light of the sun, and the light of the sun shall be sevenfold, as the light of seven days, in the day that the Lord bindeth up the breach of his people, and healeth the stroke of their wound" (Isaiah 30:26).

That will be true daylight saving time.

Production, under the new climate condition and superb growing conditions, will be fantastic. *Energy needs will be solved.*

Evidently the unconverted will have a hundred years *probation* in which to adjust to the righteous rule of Christ and His saints. After this, if they have not yielded, they will be removed.

"He shall judge the poor of the people, he shall save the children of the needy, and shall break in pieces the oppressor" (Psalm 72:4).

There will be no place for exorbitant interest rates.

There will be social justice for all.

No loafing or welfare moonlighting will be permitted.

Offenders will be dealt with summarily.

CHRIST, THE TRUE PONTIFEX-MAXIMUS

Many in history have sought the role of priest-king, combining the roles of God and government. Caesar sought it. Hitler sought it. It is the dream of hell. Usurpers have tried and tumbled.

This role belongs to Jesus. "Yet have I set my King upon my holy hill of Zion" (Psalm 2:6).

Melchizedek, in the dawn of recorded history, foreshadowed this role to be incarnated in Jesus of Nazareth. "And Melchizedek king of Salem brought forth bread and wine: and he was priest of the most high God" (Genesis 14:18). "Whither the forerunner is for us entered, even Jesus, made an high priest for ever after the order of Melchizedek" (Hebrews 6:20).

Jesus will share this greatest of all offices with His saints. "And hath made us kings and priests unto God and his Father; to him be the glory and dominion for ever and ever. Amen" (Revelation 1:6).

God intended that Israel should be a nation of priests, a kingdom of saints, "And ye shall be unto me a kingdom of priests, and a holy nation. These are the words which thou shalt speak unto the children of Israel" (Exodus 19:6).

God intends the Church to fill the same role. "Ye also, as lively stones, are built up a spiritual house, a holy priesthood, to offer up spiritual sacrifices, acceptable to God by Jesus Christ" (1 Peter 2:5). Peter emphasizes the fact. "But ye are a chosen generation, a royal priesthood, a holy nation, a peculiar people; that ye should show forth the praises of him who hath called you out of darkness into his marvelous light: which in time past were not a people, but are now the people of God: which had not obtained mercy, but now have obtained mercy" (1 Peter 2:9,10).

This identifies the work of the believer during the Millennium. His spiritual character and ministry fit him to exercise government-management in any sphere of life upon earth to which Christ assigns him.

SATAN'S LAST HURRAH

"And when the thousand years are expired, Satan shall be loosed out of his prison" (Revelation 20:7).

It is for a short season.

The purpose is to prove that *birth*, not environment, determines nature.

Putting a pig into a parlor doesn't change the pig. Millions, living under millennial reign, submit and serve only because they must. They turn toward Satan at their first opportunity.

Satan "shall go out to deceive." Jesus said that Satan is a "liar" and "a murderer." *This will be his final harvest.* "To gather them together to battle: the number of whom is as the sand of the sea" (Revelation 20:8).

"And fire came down from God out of heaven, and devoured them. And the devil that deceived them was cast into the lake of fire and brimstone, where the beast and the false prophet are, and shall be tormented day and night for ever and ever" (Revelation 20:9,10).

All three receive life sentences for premeditated assault and murder.

AN INTERESTING PERIOD

The Millennium is not an age of consummation, nor is it final perfection. Men will die, children will be born, evil will exist in many hearts, though disobedience will not be permitted.

It is humanity's last probation.

What is "Gog and Magog"?

They are names borrowed from Ezekiel to describe people who are opposed to God and His saints.

Mankind retains the freedom of *choice.*

That is important to the understanding of these "one thousand years."

What happened in Eden will happen at the close of the Millennium. Satan will *deceive.* An imperfect heart toward God and righteousness will accept deception. It takes God, not genes, to make a saint out of a sinner.

What about God's people who rule with Christ?

They will not be deceived. They have already received immortality and incorruptible bodies. These bodies can never be touched by sin, decay, or death.

It is noteworthy to observe that God establishes a true and workable United Nations for the thousand-year period. Earth's nations will share in the heritage of Israel by taking part in the Feast of Tabernacles, thus declaring that they are led by the Lord just as Israel was led in the wilderness.

"And it shall come to pass, that every one that is left of all the nations which came against Jerusalem, shall even go up from year to year to worship the King, the Lord of hosts, and to keep the feast of tabernacles. And it shall be, that whoso will not come up of all the families of the earth unto Jerusalem to worship the King, the Lord of hosts, even upon them there shall be no rain" (Zechariah 14:16,17).

Those are *sanctions—drought—*that will work. Every body mankind has tried to organize has not been able to enforce the will of that organization. That weakness is overcome in the Millennium.

12 The Final Audit

There must be a *final audit*.

Everyone intuitively believes it.

The price of privilege is *responsibility*.

"And as it is appointed unto man once to die, but after this the judgment" (Hebrews 9:27).

"And whosoever was not found written in the book of life was cast into the lake of fire" (Revelation 20:15).

God is bigger than I am.

Are we prepared? There were those in Israel, who talked freely about God's day and what it would be like, who were more unprepared than those they contemplated coming to judgment. "Woe unto you that desire the day of the Lord! to what end is it for you? the day of the Lord [for you] is darkness, and not light" (Amos 5:18).

Religious appearances are not enough.

No one can outmatch his Creator. None have. That is the stubborn story of history. There have been many robust, audacious sinners. All have succumbed.

Trials for the wicked are held *after* the one-thousand-years period. This is described in Revelation 20. "But the rest of the dead lived not again until the thousand years were finished. . . . And I saw the dead, small and great, stand before God; and the books were opened: and another book was opened, which is the book of life: and the dead were judged out of those things which were written in the books, according to their works" (Revelation 20:5,12).

Just as all the righteous must appear before the judgment seat of Christ *before* the Millennium, so all the wicked must appear before the Great White Throne after the Millennium.

There are no exceptions.

God gave Solomon wisdom. Lust provided opportunity for Satan. Satan deceived Solomon. Solomon thought he was an exception, that he could get by. Then his kingdom began to fall part. His problems multiplied. His sorrows grew. Solomon concluded before his death, "Fear God, and keep his commandments: for this is the whole duty of man. For God shall bring every work into judgment, with every secret thing, whether it be good, or whether it be evil" (Ecclesiastes 12:13,14).

Satan persuades mankind that God doesn't mean it, that it is only a bluff. Judgment is as sure as death.

RIGHTEOUS JUDGMENT

God is no respecter of persons.

"Wherefore now let the fear of the Lord be upon you; take heed and do it: for there is no iniquity with the Lord our God, nor respect of persons, nor taking of gifts" (2 Chronicles 19:7).

God cannot be *bribed*.

"For the Lord your God is God of gods, and Lord of lords, a great God, a mighty, and a terrible, which regardeth not persons, nor taketh reward" (Deuteronomy 10:17).

Mankind will not be judged by rank, success, achievement, or reputation. They will be weighed!

"Thou art weighed in the balances, and art found wanting" (Daniel 5:27).

Joseph A. Seiss comments on the One presiding, "an awful, mysterious, and composed presence, which can be nothing less than the one unnameable, indescribable, eternal Godhead. If He were the Lord Jesus Christ simply as the God-man, He would appear in some definite form as in every other instance."

"And I saw a great white throne, and him that sat on it, from whose face the earth and the heaven fled away; and there was found no place for them" (Revelation 20:11).

Each case will have been fully investigated and fully documented. "They were judged every man according to their works" (Revelation 20:13).

Isaiah warns, that the Lord, "shall not judge after the sight of his eyes, neither reprove after the hearing of his ears" (11:3). He is omniscient. He, who created the atom, is Master of detail. "Shall not the Judge of all the earth do right" (Genesis 18:25)?

Nevertheless the books will be opened. Every extenuating circumstance will be recorded. "If thou, Lord, shouldest mark iniquities, O Lord, who shall stand? But there is forgiveness with thee, that thou mayest be feared" (Psalm 130:3,4). Calvary is the one answer to judgment. My faith in His substitution covers it all.

The unrepentant will find his deeds accuse him. I am never good *enough*. I am not totally truthful. I am not completely generous. I am not absolutely pure. "For all have sinned, and come short of the glory of God" (Romans 3:23). *I am judged by that middle cross, not against the thieves on either side.* "Neither is there salvation in any other: for there is none

114

other name under heaven given among men, whereby we must be saved" (Acts 4:12).

Your favorite denomination cannot save you.

"And the Lord said unto Moses, Whosoever hath sinned against me, him will I blot out of my book" (Exodus 32:33).

THE SECOND DEATH

There is a maximum security penitentiary for the ages.

"The fearful, and the unbelieving, and the abominable, and murderers, and whoremongers, and sorcerers, and idolators, and all liars, shall have their part in the lake which burneth with fire and brimstone: which is the second death" (Revelation 21:8).

It is interesting to note that the "fearful, and unbelieving" head this "Most Wanted" list. All that is needed to confine you forever is to be "fearful." "And I was afraid, and went and hid thy talent. . . . His lord answered and said unto him, Thou wicked and slothful servant. . . . Cast ye the unprofitable servant into outer darkness: there shall be weeping and gnashing of teeth" (Matthew 25:25,26,30).

You are either *for* or *against*. There can be no middle ground, no playing both ends toward the middle, no "I . . . hid thy talent in the earth: lo, there thou hast that is thine" (Matthew 25:25).

Man's choice is man's destiny.

"The Lord is . . . not willing that any should perish, but that all should come to repentance" (2 Peter 3:9). It is said of Judas, "Judas by transgression fell, that he might go to his own place" (Acts 1:25).

God simply accommodates *your* choice.

No One Likes Bad News

King Ahab listened to the counsel of false prophets because they uttered pleasant things. He didn't want the truth. So he disliked the preacher (1 Kings 22). Paul says it will grow worse toward the end. "For the time will come when they will not endure sound doctrine; but after their own lusts shall they heap to themselves teachers, having itching ears" (2 Timothy 4:3).

It seems there is something in unregenerate nature that wants to be deceived. The Spartans of ancient Greece recognized this, and to keep the peace, they ruled that no man should tell his brother any bad news, but that everyone should be left to find it out for himself.

Paul did not follow that course. He faithfully warned. "I have not shunned to declare unto you all the counsel of God" (Acts 20:27). He said, "Knowing therefore the terror of the Lord, we persuade men" (2 Corinthians 5:11).

Nothing is so apostate as a false view of God's love.

Suppose a loving father saw his child taken by a deadly, contagious disease. Would he not separate that child from other children in order to keep the disease from spreading? Then, if the child refused the remedy it might lead to a more permanent separation. *Sin is a disease.* It is contagious and fatal.

The "second death" is total separation.

An unrepentant, unredeemed sinner in heaven would be unhappy. A sinner would immediately endeavor to turn the "city" toward licensed "palaces of sin" with bars, bookies, and brothels. "He that is unjust, let him be unjust still: and he which is filthy, let him be filthy still" (Revelation 22:11).

If you don't *enjoy* it here, sir, you won't enjoy it there.

The unbeliever loves to peddle the hypothesis that there is too much good in men for God to send anyone into the lake of fire.

Man's justice doesn't think so.

A murderer may have done many good things in his life, but a few minutes of evil will mean life imprisonment or death for him. A father may hold a glass of milk. In it are several drops of strychnine. It might be 99 percent pure milk. Would a loving father say, "There is too much good milk in this glass for me to throw it away. I will give it to my children?" Sin is poison. If sin were allowed in heaven it would make it hell. There is one antidote. "The blood of Jesus Christ his Son cleanseth us from all sin" (1 John 1:7).

"Depart from me, all ye workers of iniquity" (Luke 13:27).

Is It a Real Place?

Yes.

If hell isn't real, neither is heaven. Jesus stated both to be a fact.

The "lake of fire" is not purgatory. It is not for purification. It is punishment.

The fires of punishment cannot have more power and authority than Calvary. Punishment is not regenerative. It can restrain, but it cannot transform.

T. DeWitt Talmage wrote: "The prospect of reformation in another world is more improbable than here. Do you realize that a man starts out in this world with innocence of infancy? Starting in the next world, he starts with the accumulated bad habits of a lifetime. Is it not to be expected that you can

117

build a better ship out of a new timber than out of an old hulk? If, starting with comparative infancy, a man does not become godly, is it possible that starting with sin a seraph can be evolved? Is there not more prospect that a sculptor will make a finer statue out of a block of pure white marble than out of a black rock that has been cracked and twisted and split and scarred with the storms of half a century? And yet there are those who are so nonsensical as to believe that a man who starts in this world with infancy and its innocence and turns out badly in the next world can start as a dead failure and turn out well."

The Bible does not speak of *temporary punishment*.

It speaks of eternal punishment.

"Then shall he say also unto them on the left hand, Depart from me, ye cursed, into everlasting fire, prepared for the devil and his angels" (Matthew 25:41).

That fire is "unquenchable."

"Whose fan is in his hand, and he will thoroughly purge his floor, and will gather the wheat into his garner; but the chaff he will burn with fire unquenchable" (Luke 3:17).

The Bible does not teach *the annihilation of the wicked*.

It is true that 2 Thessalonians 1:9 does use the word "destruction." However the word is used in other passages to mean ruin or punishment. The verse goes on to tell us of what this everlasting punishment consists. It is "from [literally, away from] the presence of the Lord, and from the glory of his power." It is final separation from God. That is the hell of hells.

The final death that is the penalty for sin is not

physical death or the cessation of existence. It is separation from God and the blessings of God-consciousness.

The Moment God Takes You at Your Word

Time after time you have responded to God's invitation, "Leave me alone!" Think! Do you mean it? The "second death" is God finally taking you at your word. That is *your* choice, not *His*.

God wanted *sons*, not puppets or automatons. So God created man with free will. Love cannot be forced. It must be freely given. There must be *response*. There is a vast difference between the doll that cries "Mama," and the child who approaches without guile and says, "I love you."

For choice to be genuine, God had to permit the possibility that man might make the wrong choice, and reject His love.

God blockades the path to destruction.

These agents work to say within the prodigal, "I will arise and go to my father, and will say unto him, Father, I have sinned against heaven, and before thee" (Luke 15:18):

The Holy Spirit
The prayers of God's people
The Church
The Bible
Jesus Christ
The providences of God
Conscience

If you persist in running through every stoplight, you must pay the consequences.

The sense of *guilt* is a heavy burden.

13 Everything's Coming Up New

"And he that sat upon the throne said, Behold, I make all things new" (Revelation 21:5).

This is not *renovation*.

This is a new *conception*.

Isaiah 65:17, "For, behold, I create new heavens and a new earth: and the former shall not be remembered, nor come into mind," uses a Hebrew word indicating an unprecedented creation that will in no way remind us of the present earth and heavens.

That is why there shall be "no more sea."

The first creation was good because it was perfectly suited to God's purposes. The new conception will also be good, perfectly suited to the final expression of God's purpose.

Fire—a mighty blast—will bring to an end what has been explored, photographed, charted, appropriated. "The heavens shall pass away with a great noise, and the elements shall melt with fervent heat, the earth also and the works that are therein shall be burned up" (2 Peter 3:10).

Everything contaminated by rebellion and sin shall be erased. "Then cometh the end, when he shall have delivered up the kingdom to God, even the Father; when he shall have put down all rule, and all authority and power. For he must reign, till he hath put all enemies under his feet. The last enemy that shall be destroyed is death. For he hath put all things under his feet. But when he saith, All things are put under him, it is manifest that he is excepted, which did put all things under him. And when all things shall be subdued unto him, then shall the Son also himself be subject unto him that put all things under him, that God may be all in all" (1 Corinthians 15:24-28).

The new concept without ocean area is suited to a new creation and purpose.

The sea is often used to picture *unrest.* "The wicked are like the troubled sea, when it cannot rest" (Isaiah 57:20).

The sea is a simile for *grief.* "There is sorrow on the sea; it cannot be quiet" (Jeremiah 49:23).

Unrest and grief will be unknown. There will be neither agitation nor mystery.

The sea is used to describe *rebellion.* "And upon the earth distress of nations, with perplexity; the sea and the waves roaring" (Luke 21:25).

Former conditions—distances, barriers, storms—will be unknown.

The Creator has a new idea.

The New City

The city that God showed to Abraham, in vision, will be ready for unveiling. The story is from blueprint to ribbon-cutting. "For he looked for a city which hath foundations, whose builder and maker is God" (Hebrews 11:10). Occupancy is a coveted honor. "But now they desire a better country, that is, a heavenly: wherefore God is not ashamed to be called their God: for he hath prepared for them a city" (Hebrews 11:16).

John was given a preview. "And he carried me away in the spirit to a great and high mountain, and showed me that great city, the holy Jerusalem, descending out of heaven from God" (Revelation 21:10).

You can't have a city without inhabitants.

It takes organization and dwelling places to make inhabitants something more than a crowd. Thus, "the bride, the Lamb's wife," the great body of faithful believers of all ages will have their home and headquarters in the eternal city, the New Jerusalem.

The city, too, is a new conception.

It will be the epitome of *beauty*.

It will be of "pure gold, like unto clear glass" (Revelation 21:18).

The Bible is using human language to try to describe some substance that is entirely different from anything we know in building materials today. Its splendor and radiance will go beyond even that of gold and will partake of the radiance of the most precious metals we know.

The city will be laid out as a square measuring 12,000 furlongs (1,378 English miles) to the side. Its walls of jasper will be 144 cubits (210 feet) high (Revelation 21:12,17,18). Because the height of the outside wall is definitely stated along with the height of the city, it may be better to describe the contour of the city as *pyramidal*.

The wall will have 12 foundation stones, each adorned with a specific type of precious stone. The first level will feature diamonds; the second with rich, blue lapis lazuli; the third with blue-green chalcedony; the fourth with bright, green emeralds; the fifth with red-layered sardonyx; the sixth with deep red carnelian; the seventh with yellow topaz; the eighth with sea-green beryl; the ninth with rich, yellow-green peridot; the tenth with apple-green chrysoprasus; the eleventh with blue hyacinth stones; the twelfth with rich, clear purple amethyst.

What dazzling brilliance!

On each stratum of foundation will be engraved the name of one of the 12 apostles. There will be 12 gates, three on each side of the city, and each made of a single, giant pearl. The gates will have the names of the 12 tribes of Israel written on them. At each gate an angel will be stationed, and the gate will be open always, for there will be no night (Revelation 21:12, 13,21,25).

JESUS WILL OUTSHINE IT ALL

The beauty of Christ's personality transcends all. Heaven is a suitable framework for Jesus of Nazareth. The eternal society is built around Him.

God created man as a social being, with the ability to communicate. God said, "It is not good that man should be alone" (Genesis 2:18). Yet the eternal world will have *a new basis,* a new social structure. "For when they shall rise from the dead, they neither marry, nor are given in marriage; but are as the angels which are in heaven" (Mark 12:25). Happiness and personal fulfillment will be in God. We have a foretaste of this now. "Which is the earnest of our inheritance until the redemption of the purchased possession, unto the praise of his glory" (Ephesians 1:14).

The Spirit-filled walk draws the Spirit-filled close in fellowship, in kindred ties, to the fellow believer.

If this affords us pleasure, how much greater must be the rapture of companionship in the New Jerusalem with those for whom we have perfect love in the Lord!

No defects will cause sorrow.

No lack of wisdom will blight affections or break friendships.

There will be no objectionable faults.

Nothing will detract.

There will be no break in friendships.

Instead of the bitterness, petty dislikes, and terrifying hatreds of this world, there will be perfect peace and brotherly love. Every person will be stalwart, fine, unselfish, understanding, and friendly.

Pure Joy

Now death is king. "Nevertheless death reigned from Adam to Moses, even over them that had not sinned after the similitude of Adam's trangsgression, who is the figure of him that was to come" (Romans 5:14). The king of terrors will be dethroned.

There will be no cemeteries.

There will be no hospitals.

There will be no mortuaries.

There will be no reason for sorrow or weeping.

Pain will vanish.

Here pain serves a purpose. It warns us of danger. It purifies character. It genders sympathy. It helps us appreciate Christ's sufferings.

None of the effects of sin will ever be seen, for sin will never touch or taint the new creature.

There will be "no more curse."

No one will be *hungry*.

No one will be cold.

No one will be joined to an emaciated, or crippled, or embarrassed body.

There will be a new "front page."

A PREPARED PEOPLE

"He that overcometh shall inherit all things; and I will be his God, and he shall be my son" (Revelation 21:7).

Character begins here.

"Our conversation is in heaven" (Philippians 3:20). Our dialogue is not with a world system.

"Love not the world, neither the things that are in the world. If any man love the world, the love of the Father is not in him. For all that is in the world, the lust of the flesh, and the lust of the eyes, and the pride of life, is not of the Father, but is of the world. And the world passeth away, and the lust thereof: but he that doeth the will of God abideth for ever" (1 John 2:15-17).

Moffatt's translation of Philippians 3:20 is "We are a colony of heaven." As colonists our business is to reproduce the manners, laws, customs, and institutions of the mother country in the land where we have been placed.

Our directive is to do God's will on earth.

"Let your light so shine before men, that they may see your good works, and glorify your Father which is in heaven" (Matthew 5:16).

The reward is to the *overcomer.*

This check should never be forgotten by either pulpit or pew.

Cowardly compromisers; unbelieving rejecters of the gospel; abominable persons polluted with pride, selfishness, and deceit; murderers; sexually immoral persons of all kinds; sorcerers who bewitch people and take away their dignity and personal freedom by drugs, poisons, philosophies; idolaters; and all liars who accept and propagate Satan's lies will never see the gates of the New World.

God has no intention of approving any form of heaven-hell amalgamation.

A FULL AND COMPLETE LIFE

"And his servants shall serve him: and they shall see his face; and his name shall be in their foreheads" (Revelation 22:3,4).

We shall always be *individuals*.

Yet we will be totally dependent upon God. There will be full provision. "For the Lord God giveth them light" (Revelation 22:5).

Heaven is not a place where "retired choir members bore each other with bad singing." *Heaven is a place of meaningful employment.* God has always given man work to do. We shall have a new creation to explore and adapt. "But as it is written, Eye hath not seen, nor ear heard, neither have entered into the heart of man, the things which God hath prepared for them that love him" (1 Corinthians 2:9).

Knowledge will be unlimited. "For now we see through a glass, darkly, but then face to face: now I know in part; but then shall I know even as also I am known" (1 Corinthians 13:12).

The New Jerusalem will have no church buildings of any kind.

Their purpose here is to suggest a sanctuary where God's presence is manifest. In the New World His presence sanctifies all areas. No special day of worship is needed. There will be no need of ritual, for every act will be "holiness unto the Lord."

Imagine the perfect occupation, the perfect garden, the perfect music, the perfect society, perfect friends, perfect art, and all the *perfection* that spirit, mind, and body can ever desire. That is *glory*.

And it will be worth it.